Celtic Warrior Descendants

Celtic Warrior Descendants

A Genetic and Cultural History
of a Rural American Family

by
Ebe Chandler McCabe, Jr.

iUniverse, Inc.
Bloomington

Celtic Warrior Descendants
A Genetic and Cultural History of a Rural American Family

Copyright © 2011 Ebe Chandler McCabe, Jr.

All rights reserved. No part of this book may be used or reproduced by any means, graphic, electronic, or mechanical, including photocopying, recording, taping or by any information storage retrieval system without the written permission of the publisher except in the case of brief quotations embodied in critical articles and reviews.

iUniverse books may be ordered through booksellers or by contacting:

iUniverse
1663 Liberty Drive
Bloomington, IN 47403
www.iuniverse.com
1-800-Authors (1-800-288-4677)

Because of the dynamic nature of the Internet, any web addresses or links contained in this book may have changed since publication and may no longer be valid. The views expressed in this work are solely those of the author and do not necessarily reflect the views of the publisher, and the publisher hereby disclaims any responsibility for them.

Any people depicted in stock imagery provided by Thinkstock are models, and such images are being used for illustrative purposes only.

Certain stock imagery © Thinkstock.

ISBN: 978-1-4502-9364-8 (pbk)

Library of Congress Control Number: 2011901495

Printed in the United States of America

iUniverse rev. date: 3/14/11

Contents

Dedication

This is a different kind of family history/genealogy, with a different kind of dedication–to those whom its contents are intended to benefit–in order of ascending importance:

- Family genealogists/historians interested in providing a deeper legacy and a more realistic perspective.

- American descendants of western Europeans, whose ancestors made their Celtic culture and genes pervasive in that part of the world, and especially those descendants who know little about their deeper ancestral culture.

- My genetic and cultural family, particularly those who are unaware of how typically American their genes, ancestry and culture are. Among these are my stepdaughter Lisa and my step-grandson Christopher. Culturally, they are members of my family; genetically, their ancestry parallels mine in leading back to a common ethnicity among my direct patrilineal (male) ancestors and their corresponding matrilineal (female line) ones.

- My son Keith and my grandson KC. Keith grew up, after the age of 10, over half the country away from me, and KC has never lived near me. My hope is that this work will provide some compensation for the consequent lack of paternal and grandparental presence and input.

Acknowledgments

My father often delved into his memory to figure out if and how people were related. His brother *Jim* had an even more avid interest in family. I wasn't interested until my stepdaughter fascinated me with the idea of writing a family history to counter the information loss incident to the passing of each generation. The following individuals enabled that to happen.

My brother, Harley William (Hap) McCabe, of Salisbury, Maryland. Hap corrected a lot of my mistakes and added valuable memories of his own.

My 1st cousin, Barbara Rickards Godwin of Millsboro, Delaware. Barbara contributed a huge amount of information about the Chandler and McCabe families.

My 1st cousin, Marvin Pascoe, whose widow Billye provided information Marvin had collected on the Coulis family.

My 3rd cousin, Cassandra (Sandie) Gerken of Dagsboro, Delaware. Sandie provided a plenitude of meticulously researched Chandler and McCabe family information.

My 3rd Cousin, once removed, Robert (Bobby) S. Collins, Jr. of Raleigh, North Carolina. Bobby convinced me of the sincerity of the founders of Christ's Sanctified Holy Church.

My 5th cousin, Vernon McCabe of Ocean City, Maryland. Vernon's work provided a wealth of information about *John McCabe (1727-1800)* and his descendants.

My 5th cousin, once removed, Lawrence (Larry) Rettinger of Kerrville, Texas. Larry provided valuable information on *1727 John McCabe* and on *Josiah Campbell*.

My 5th cousin, once removed, and high school friend and classmate Carl Schulz of Plant City, Florida. Carl showed me how to begin this work.

My 5th cousin, once removed, and high school classmate Betty McComrick Walker of Rehoboth Beach, Delaware. Betty contributed from her many years of Bible study.

Brunhildi (Bruni) Wais Mecabe, of Jackonville, Florida. Bruni was the prime information source on the Mecabe branch of the family.

Mrs. Eliot Marshall of Yardley, Pennsylvania. Her perceptive comments resulted in major improvement of the scope and extent of this history.

Mrs. Justine Opaleski of Yardley, Pennsylvania. Her comments helped the organization and style of this history considerably.

Mr. Fritz Marston of Ewing, NJ. His advice on finishing up this work and preparing it for publication were invaluable.

Many other direct and indirect contributors cannot practicably be listed here. But I am deeply thankful for every one of them.

Preface

This book began as a family genealogy. It became a mini-history of much more, including two sincere religious groups in a dispute over sexual behavior. Manslaughter resulted. The killer got off because his supporters blamed the peaceable sect. I hope that this work satisfies the cousin who asked me, over a hundred years later: How did they get away with that?

Genealogy showed that my family is Celtic (pronounced Keltic), as are other American families descended from western European ancestors. We're not solely Celtic because America really is a melting pot, but we have a common Celtic background. So I flavored this work with a taste of Celtic folklore.

The Celts[1] were superior warriors, iron workers, farmers, and artisans (who made marvelous gold jewelry and ornamental weapons). They invented ring armor. Their culture was a central/western European one. Its roots go back to the 2400 BC Beaker folk, makers of pottery beakers/urns having an inverted bell-shaped profile. Next came the Early Bronze Age Unĕtice Culture noted for its metal work, then the Middle Bronze Age Tumulus Culture that buried their dead under mounds, and then the Late Bronze age Urnfield Culture that cremated its deceased and put their ashes in urns that they buried in fields. Austria's proto-Celtic, salt-mining Halstatt Culture, noted for the first appearance of iron swords, followed and expanded through much of central Europe. Out of it came the late iron age La Tène Celtic Culture, noted for its metal work. The Celtic culture extended into France, Ireland, Britain, Belgium, West Germany, southern Germany, Poland, northern Italy, the Netherlands, northern Europe, and Russia. It was the dominant central and western European culture in the first millennium BC.

DNA information took this history back past its American roots to European and earlier ones. Our Irish and British ancestors have roots in the Iberian Peninsula (Spain and Portugal), where their ancestors sheltered during the last ice age. Some early Irish and British may even have walked to the Isles before melting ice flooded the Irish Sea (keeping snakes out of Ireland) and filled the English Channel. Going back further revealed a middle eastern phase of our ancestral heritage—one that followed the emigration of our African ancestors to Europe and Asia.

While the family history was being traced, evidence kept popping up to show that our Christian culture did not just cast out preceding ones. It merged with them, as those earlier cultures had also done as they developed. The conclusion that our pagan ancestors were very much like us became inescapable.

Another inescapable conclusion was that the civics and history I learned in school did not realistically depict our ancestors' (and our) world. So I inserted some political realities learned from my parents and from personal experience, throughout the book and under the topic of Political Heritage. (Readers have an inherent right to disagree with my views.)

Information also was added to provide perspective on the family's Celtic heritage, especially its English, Irish, Scotch, and Scotch-Irish aspects. Hopefully, readers will better understand our family and cultural commonalities as a result.

This was, overall, a giant learning experience for me. I hope it also will be a bit of an education for those who wade through it.

Explanation of Charts

The genealogy charts used in this history typically use:

- Boxes to identify individuals.

- Double lines to interconnect spouses/watch-mates.

- Single lines to connect parents to their progeny/descendants.

- Mothers' maiden names, if known.

- A star (★) and/or heavier lines to identify a direct ancestor.

- Ganged boxes to identify siblings.

- Use of "b." and "d." for birth and death dates/times – to present partial information. ("c." or "~" may be used to denote approximate dates.)

- Other information as appropriate.

Below are sample charts for:

1. Adam and Eve and three children.

2. Jack Jones, his children with one spouse, and his child with a second spouse.

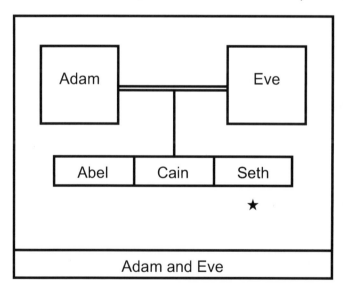

Adam and Eve

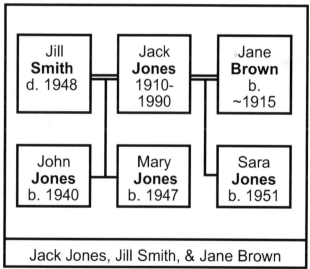

Jack Jones, Jill Smith, & Jane Brown

Notes:

1. The sample charts are illustrative; those in the history may differ.

2. Charted information might not be contained in the text.

3. Stars, where used, mark a direct line of descent.

Prologue

Basically, our families are those we care deeply about. That includes blood relatives, spouses, "significant others," children (genetic, adopted, foster and step) and their offspring, and in-laws. A former spouse is family if there are children in common. Friends can become family too. We also have families of people of similar background, education, experience, ethics, etc.

Histories are imperfect and author-biased. Some inputs are ambiguous, slanted by political correctness, colored by legend, conflicting, false, erroneously transposed, exaggerated, inaccurate, incomplete, misconstrued, or misleading. Tales vary with their hand-me-down routes. People draw different conclusions from the same inputs. Consequently, readers must judge the result. Their conclusion may be much like that of noted author/social critic E. L. Doctorow, who stated:

> *History is the present. That's why every generation writes it anew. But what most people think of as history is its end product, myth.*

Doctorow's insight is valid, but myth often has a core of truth and/or a valid moral. Rewritten history can be better than yesteryear's "truths" if throwing out the baby with the bath water and replacing one set of prejudices with another are avoided. For, as Dr. Gerda Lerner, known for creating Women's History, put it:

> *We can learn from history how past generations thought and acted, how they responded to the demands of their time and how they solved their problems. We can learn by analogy, not by example, for our circumstances will always be different than theirs were. The main thing history can teach us is that human actions have consequences and that certain choices, once made, cannot be undone. They foreclose the possibility of making other choices and thus they determine future events.*

The most important aspect of history, however, lies in philosopher and poet George Santayana's famous warning:

> *Those who do not remember history are doomed to repeat it.*

Note: This caveat is often "improved" by replacing "remember" with "learn from."

Another pertinent observation was made by Philosopher Georg Hegel:

> *The only thing we learn from history is that we learn nothing from history.*

Unfortunately, Hegel's observation is all too true: mankind continually fails to learn from mistakes and consequently repeats them.

Delmarva

Delmarva is named for the three states on its ~180 mile long, ~60 mile wide peninsula.[2] The Chesapeake Bay lies to the west, the Atlantic Ocean and the Delaware River and Bay are on the east. Rural Delmarva begins south of Wilmington, Delaware. It extends through Delaware's Kent and Sussex Counties and the Eastern Shore of Maryland and Virginia to Fisherman's Island, at the north end of the mouth of the Chesapeake Bay.

The Delmarva Peninsula is low-lying. Humidity can make its winter winds chillingly cutting. Summer's heat can be fierce, but the ocean beaches are refreshing. Fall and Winter nights can be crystal clear—beautifully showing off the moon and stars.

Ships, boats and barges were early means of transport along the Delmarva coast and inland canals. Frankford, Delaware once relied on the Vine's Branch Canal to the Indian River (and horse-drawn wagons) to take goods in and out. It wasn't until the 1870s that the railroad came.[3] When Ford began producing over a million cars a year in 1921,[4] rural Delmarva's roads were still dirt, or oyster or clam shell. In Virginia, a causeway across the Chincoteague Bay made that island much more accessible in 1922.[5] In Delaware, the Dupont family provided, and donated, a paved highway the length of the state in 1924.[6] The Chesapeake Bay Bridge from Maryland's Eastern Shore to western Maryland replaced a ferry in 1952,[7] and the Chesapeake Bay Bridge-Tunnel replaced the ferry across the mouth of the bay in 1964.[8]

Delmarva's early physical isolation made it self-sufficient. Cultural isolation was a side effect. Newspapers provided notably late information until telegraphy came along in the 1840s.[9] Commercial radio came into use in the 1920s,[10] and TV broadcasts became available in the 1940s and 1950s. Even then, some Rural Delaware families considered education beyond basic reading, writing, and ciphering to be a waste. Their children left school, as soon as the law allowed, to tend to corn and soybeans and chickens (the primary industry). Many of them were driving tractors, in the fields and on the roads, by the age of 10 years—and could tote 100 pound bags of chicken feed before they reached that weight themselves.

In the Revolutionary War, Virginia's 15 regiments[11] had seven Eastern Shore companies.[12] Delaware had ~4000 Continental Army soldiers, was the first state to ratify the U.S. Constitution, and had a strong Loyalist (Tory) faction that was dispersed several times by the Whig Militia.[13] Maryland was initially against separation, but fought well: George Washington reportedly esteemed its "troops of the line" and gave Maryland its "Old Line State" nickname.[14]

Chincoteague and Tangier Islands were the only parts of Virginia that did not secede from the Union.[15] Prior to the Civil War, Maryland had 87,000 slaves.[16] It didn't secede but sent 65,000 men to the Union Army and 25,000 others to the Confederacy.[17] Delaware, with 1800 slaves (and 20,000 free African-Americans) didn't secede either. Its governor stated that Delaware had been the first state to embrace the Union and would be the last to leave it. Still, some Delaware citizens served in the Confederacy, rural Delaware swung the state's vote against abolishing slavery, and the state practiced segregation and "separate but equal" education until the 1950s.[18]

The earliest depiction of rural Delmarva life I've seen is in the autobiography of *Josiah Campbell (2/18/1810-1/20/1890)*,[19] the youngest of nine children. Beehive honey and wax provided more family income than the produce grown on the sandy soil of their farm in Baltimore Hundred, which is in Lower Sussex County, Delaware. The Campbell children went to school two months a year. Each student studied and recited from his/her own book. *Josiah's* was the bible; little else was available.

Large parts of Delaware were then swamp where cedar trees were buried under decaying vegetation. The well-preserved cedars were profitable to harvest, so Josiah's family worked extensively in the swamp. Its older members did the hard work. The younger ones carried out the clap boards to dry land or to corduroy roads. (The swamp wouldn't bear the weight of laden horses or mules, and briers and bushes made it passable only on established paths.) *Josiah* typically ate the dinner he carried before starting his day's work and fasted the rest of the day.

The Campbell family's pigs roamed the swamp and were prey for bears. Weakening squealing characterized a successful bear attack. A loud squeal followed by silence meant the pig had escaped. Those animals returned with the backs of their necks torn.

Josiah found the supernatural a greater terror than the bears. He cited, as an example, an addition to the family home. The man his father sent for to "run" a stairway became ill and died en route, and the stairs were thereafter considered haunted. Hammering and sawing noises reportedly were heard from them. *Josiah* believed such stories when he lived in Delaware. He also dreaded ghosts, and shut his eyes and ran as fast as possible when passing a graveyard at night. (Some peeking may have been involved.)

William Godfrey, on old man *Josiah* knew, walked lamely because of a running sore at the hip joint–the reputed result of being shot by a silver bullet fired by a witch. But he worked in the swamp all week. On Saturdays he and *Josiah* went fishing. *William* was said to bewitch his bait so the fish would take it, and his every cast seemed to produce a catch. So *Josiah* would leave his unproductive spot and drop his line in near William's, whereupon the fish stopped biting. *William* then ceded the spot to *Josiah* and moved. At the end of the day, he divided his full bucket with *Josiah*, and they both went home happy.

Josiah moved to Ohio as a young man, and married. He then came to realize how superstitious the people of Delaware were, but that didn't eradicate his own superstitions. On a visit to lower Sussex County's Baltimore Hundred in his later years, he was walking with his wife past a graveyard, describing the place as being where ghosts had been seen. Suddenly, they heard rustling and saw bushes shaking. *Josiah* was inclined to feel that a ghost was on top of them. (His wife wouldn't admit to believing that.) They initially saw nobody, but eventually found the cause to be a little girl gathering huckleberry bushes to make a broom for sweeping yards.

Delmarva's isolation was evident in a September 1894 newspaper article.[20] The author, Rudolph Block, noted that the 244 miles from New York City to Chincoteague was normally about a six hour journey (to somewhere else). But his trip to Chincoteague became slow and painful after reaching Wilmington, Delaware. It took nine hours to reach Franklin City, Virginia, and the trip across Chincoteague Bay to the island was made the next day.

Block wrote that most Chincoteague Islanders were born there and lived exactly as their forefathers did 100 years earlier. Many had never been to the mainland. They were reportedly prone to violence but very religious.[21] Their "only textbook" was the Bible. Most oystermen carried a copy. All the Islanders could "quote more lines from it and quote them with greater accuracy than the ordinary scholar." They prayed on arising in the morning and before retiring at night. Grace was said before each meal. When the oyster fleet sailed, "a thousand prayers" were made for its safe return. Work ended at sunset on Saturday and little was heard but prayers and hymns until Monday.

One windless night, Block watched the oyster fleet drift with the tide. Calm water reflected their lights like a mirror. They were close enough to hear the oystermen sing a hymn. That "infinitely sweet" sound was "mellowed by the distance" and fell with "wonderful pathos" on "that lonely coast, under the vaulted, starry sky."

Block asked an Islander who had not been to the mainland if he had seen a locomotive or streetcar. The man answered: *"No, sir, an' what's mo', I hain't had 'ny cur'osity t' see 'em. They be n't in my line. My line's oysterin', sir, an lokymotors 'n streetkyahs hain't got nuthin t' do with oysterin."*

My father grew up in Frankford, Delaware during the first years of the 20th Century. Farming, especially strawberries and corn, was the primary industry then. *Dad* attended a one-room school. His family commuted on horseback to the family farm. Snow fell before Thanksgiving and stayed on the ground until April, and the people ice skated and drove horse-drawn sleds.

Dad moved us to Frankford in 1943. By then the town had shrunk to ~400 people. Some trains still had a passenger car. There was one Methodist and one Presbyterian church. One of the four grocery stores was relatively modern, the others were representative of General Stores of days soon past. Truitt's Store, one of the older ones, was next to the first house we moved into, and sat next to the sidewalk. It had a porch-like roof extending to the edge of the street, supported by pump pipe that was fun to shinny up. There were two gasoline pumps at the sidewalk's edge. Each had a big, graduated, cylindrical glass jar at the top. Gas was hand-pumped to fill the jar to the ordered amount, using a lever on the side of the pump assembly, with the hose used to drain the gas into the customer's tank by gravity. In good weather old-timers sat on the two wooden benches placed across the store front and told stories. At other times, they sat inside near the pickle barrel, toward the back of the store. Their other hangout was *Charlie Franklin's* Barber Shop, where they played checkers and gossiped.

Frankford's firehouse had a battered pool table in a back room and a one-room town library with an outside access. The town bank was next door. Across the street was a grave monument business. A specialty store close to the railroad sold fountain pens and stationery. Another one-room store, near my great-grandfather's house, sold candy in big showcases. (Their licorice blocks, shaped to mimic cut-plug chewing tobacco, were delicious.) A small store next to the Post Office sold newspapers and magazines. The town physician, *Dr. Long*, a cum laude graduate of Yale Medical School, ran the practice his father and grandfather had run before him, and made house calls. Frankford also had a dry cleaner, a filling station with electric motor-operated gas pumps (and a 5¢ pinball machine), a fertilizer factory, and a poultry factory. Its African-American community was physically and socially separate. Their homes looked small and poor. (Dagsboro, the next town to the north, had no minority community then. African-Americans reportedly weren't allowed there after sunset until they were permitted to attend the Clayton Theater beginning about 1950.[22])

Chicken farming became the primary industry in Sussex County. Poultry feed stores abounded. Their owners often raised chickens too–hiring families to do the work. Some of those families lived on the upper floor of a two-story section in the middle of a long, narrow, one-story chicken house, with a storeroom for chicken feed directly below them. These "residences," some partitioned, some just a common room, are gone now. So are the rows of even smaller one-room shanties that housed many of the poultry factory's African-American workers.

Today's Frankford is a small residential community–no doctor, no grocery store, no train station, no candy store, etc. Centralization (e.g., Purdue Industries in Salisbury, Maryland) has taken over the poultry industry.

Snow is now rare in Delmarva. Its seashore is thriving. The land is increasing in value. Vacation and retirement homes are proliferating–even away from the beaches.

Delmarva's Earliest People

Delmarva's earliest people were Indians, most of them tribes of the Algonquins.[23] The Assateague, the Nanticoke, and the Pocomoke are fairly well known tribal names. But there were also the Choptanks, Manokins, Wicomicoes, and many others.[24]

Captain John Smith (of Jamestown, Virginia, befriended by Pocahontas) sailed up the Nanticoke River while exploring the Chesapeake Bay in 1608. He tried to put a boat ashore. It was met by Nanticoke Indian arrows, and withdrew. The next morning, the Indians showed up with baskets of food. Muskets were fired over their heads. They ran off, and warriors were seen to have been lying in ambush in the reeds. Later that day, Smith went ashore. No Indians were found, but glass beads, copper beads, and shells left as gifts were. The next day, four Indians approached Smith's ship by canoe. He convinced them of his friendship. Then, supplies from the ship were traded for food, water and furs, and several Nanticokes guided Smith's exploration of the river.[25]

Delmarva's Indians grew corn, beans, squash, sunflowers, and tobacco.[26] The Nanticoke caught clams, crabs, eels, fish, oysters, and shrimp, using nets, spears, and weirs. They ate corn as a vegetable or made it into meal. Pone bread was made from a cornmeal and water mix baked on flat, fire-heated stones. Silk grass, bulrush, corn husks, hemp, bark and cones were used to make baskets.. Winter clothing was worn with its bear or deer fur next to the skin. Warm weather garments had the fur scraped off. Deer skin was used for moccasins, leggings, cloaks and robes.[27] The Pocomoke were farmers, hunters, trappers, and watermen on the Chesapeake Bay and the surrounding wetlands. They grew squash and corn, and hunted bear, deer, elk, rabbits, racoons, and waterfowl. Both the Pocomoke and Nanticoke made their own money out of shells and amber.[28]

Delmarva's European settlers learned much about surviving off the land and water from the Indians. But there was serious friction. Colonel Edward Scarburgh, a Virginian, campaigned to rid the Maryland-Virginia area of Indians. When Maryland refused him aid, he began what was known as the "Seaside War" of 1659 on his own. It failed because the Indians just disappeared into the marshes.

Indian treaties with Maryland didn't work. Colonists let their cattle into Indian cornfields, broke their traps, cut their timber, took their lands without authorization, and stole from the tombs of Indian kings. When a plot for a general uprising "fomented" by the Shawnee Chief Messowan was discovered, the provincial government dissolved the Indian empire, making each Indian community separate. By the end of the decade, the initially friendly Assateague[29] (and most other tribes) had left Delmarva, emigrating to the north. An Assateague tribal remnant lives near the Indian River in Delaware. Little of its native culture remains. A few Nanticoke of mixed blood also live on the Indian River.[30]

The Indians' alertness and elusiveness forestalled the worst efforts of Scarburgh and his kind. There were no massacres of or by these Indians who, divided and conquered, delayed the end of their way of life by leaving their homeland.

The Neighbors

When we moved from Frankford to a farm about a mile away, we met *Mr. George Washington Murray*, who lived nearby (alongside the then two-lane Dupont Highway) with his wife, *Miss Addie*, and his younger daughter, *Josephine* (*Josie*).

Mr. Murray's older daughter, *Olive*, lived with her husband, *David McDade*, and their son in the next house along the highway to the north. I remember *Mr. McDade* mostly for his Chesapeake Bay Retriever and his virulent Republican politics. The dog was mean and the politics were derogatory toward President Truman. We admired *"Give 'em Hell Harry"* and didn't like *Mr. McDade's* vehement opposition.

Josie married a coast guardsman, *Pat Patterson*. They had three children, *Jane, Georgie Reed, and Mark*. *Pat* and *Josie* settled in Sussex County, and *Georgie Reed* is now the pastor at the church my brother attends in Salisbury, Maryland.

Mr. Murray and *Miss Addie* soon became strong family friends. I think of them as representative of an older rural Delmarva. *Mr. Murray* grew corn, raised chickens (10,000 at a time) and drove a school bus that he also used to deliver newly-hatched chickens (biddies) to other chicken farmers. He had a mule and, for a while, a billy goat bought to pull a small wagon for his grandson to ride in. *Miss Addie* grew chrysanthemums and helped with the chicken rearing. She had a big garden next to the driveway. An arbor, heavy with Concord Grapes in the summer, stood between the *Murray's* barn and the dirt road between our house and theirs.

I remember that grape arbor for two things. One was the grapes' taste—much sweeter than the wild blackberries down the road. The other was a visit from *Franklin* and *Norman Bunting*, the younger brothers of *Gloria*, a school classmate of mine. The *Buntings* lived less than a quarter of a mile down the Dupont Highway, across from *Wilmer Lewis'* filling station. *Norman* wasn't very old then. *Mr. Murray*, while we were all next to the grape arbor, told them he could take his teeth out. They didn't believe him. So he popped his full set of false teeth out about halfway. *Franklin* wasn't perturbed. But *Norman* lit out for home at top speed. We watched him all the way. He made it in good time for such a little fellow.

When *Mom* wanted a sidewalk from the front porch steps, alongside the driveway and up to the back door, *Mr. Murray* put it in. *Dad* bought the cement–*Mr. Murray* used his mule-drawn two-wheeled cart to get the sand, framed the sidewalk, mixed the concrete, and troweled it smooth.

Another example of *Mr. Murray's* handiness was a duck decoy he "carved" with a combination hammer-hatchet. It was more a work of art than the decoy he used it as.

Mr. Murray had a double-barreled, 12-gauge, full choke shotgun, and expected to down game with one shell. His generosity resulted in our frequently having rabbit or squirrel for dinner. (They were very tasty, quite different from the bland rabbit meat I bought in a supermarket many years later.) *Mr. Murray* also went duck hunting regularly, and once killed a deer as it jumped over a fence he was walking along. The deer was out of season and, sometimes, so were the ducks. Hunting seasons were not recognized by *Mr. Murray* and his contemporaries, who saw game as part of their food supply and hunting restrictions as violating their rights.

When television became available, *Mr. Murray* bought a set, and a metal tower taller than his house for mounting the antenna. It had to be that high to bring in the nearest station, ~100 miles away in Wilmington. The picture was often grainy or unstable. But the *Murrays'* TV quickly became a highlight. We often went over to their house to watch it with them after supper. Wrestling was the biggest attraction, and we thought the bouts were real contests. To us, the leading bad guy was Mr. Moto, a reputedly Japanese wrestler whose specialty was the "Japanese Sleeper Hold." (He made an excellent villain because anti-Japanese sentiment from WWII still prevailed.) Once Mr. Moto secured his sleeper hold around an opponent's neck, by "foul" means, the bout ended with his opponent "unconscious." *Mr. Murray* often commented that he'd like to take a short-handled pitchfork to Mr. Moto.

Our favorite combatant was Argentine Rocca, a "clean" wrestler who dextrously used his feet to apply showy holds on his opponent. Rocca usually won, but was occasionally defeated by foul tactics–after he had obviously pinned his opponent with the referee failing to count him out–and with his opponent then "cheating" to pin him while Rocca was temporarily "stunned" by "illegal" tactics applied while his opponent's corner "distracted" the referee. It all made for lively discussion and an entertaining evening, and strong feelings because the bad guys won so often. After the bouts and a snack of cake or cookies, we walked the ~50 yards home. The goodbyes at the *Murray's* door always ended with "Come over" and the response "Yes, y'all come." ('Twas a simpler time–and is a very pleasant memory.)

Mr. Murray's car was a black Dodge sedan. Delmarvans mostly bought Fords (for the perceived reliability) or Chevrolets (the bodies were considered well-built). Dodges and Plymouths were less popular. Studebakers were infrequent, and disparaged because the front and rear looked so alike. Some stepped up to a Mercury or Oldsmobile, or perhaps a Buick. Individuals often were very loyal to their choices–sticking to the same brand–for cars or tractors or TVs, or whatever.

Mr. Murray and his contemporaries watched their money carefully. They dressed simply, often in bib overalls, and wore high-topped work shoes–and looked about the same as hardscrabble farmers. But when they wanted something expensive, the money was there, though they avoided being ostentatious about it. In a sense, they lived like famed painter Pablo Picasso wanted to when he said: *I'd like to live like a poor man with lots of money.*

A benefit of chicken rearing was that the feed sacks were used for making dresses. Cloth was scarce during World War II, and each chicken feed delivery brought a search of the sacks for the prettiest patterns. (*Mom* produced some astonishingly nice-looking feed sack dresses with her treadle-operated Singer Sewing Machine.)

The garden was an important part of rural Delmarva life, and we kept enough chickens for eggs and for hatching chicks to rear for the table. An annual highlight was Fourth of July dinner, with fried chicken, pole (lima) beans and corn, green vegetables, and strawberry shortcake–all self-produced. Also, we periodically had home-made ice cream, with the kids doing the cranking and the *Murrays* in attendance. Harvesting meant jelly making and canning produce in Mason jars–an intense activity for *Mom*. That canning had a lot to do with the tastiness of our winter fare. (Except on rare occasions, store-bought canned peas still have only entered my mouth under my mother's watchful eye.)

After the first frost, families worked together for hog killing. The first time the event came to our house, *Mr. Murray* told me that: *We use everything but the squeal!* When the fire was started under the cauldron, the women went inside to avoid hearing the death squeals, the hogs were shot between the eyes with a .22-caliber rifle before their throats were slit, and the ladies returned. Sugar-curing had become the means of preserving the meat, so the smoke houses weren't used and the butchering was finished in one day. There was some waste–the bristles, body hair and intestinal contents were discarded–but just about everything else was utilized. We looked forward to fresh sausage and scrapple to go with the bright orange-yolked eggs from our uncaged chickens, and to fresh pork chops.

Mr. Murray also introduced us to fatbacks (menhaden), a type of herring. He often got a "mess" of them when they were running. They're greasy and not generally used for the table. I don't remember the taste–just that *Mr. Murray* liked them a lot. {Much later I wondered, when reporting for duty to the submarine USS Menhaden (SS 377), why anyone would name a warship for such a small fish.}

Our farm had a barn, a smoke house, three small chicken houses, and an oyster house built for shucking the oysters sold by *Mr. Bowden*, an earlier owner. The oyster shells were our driveway. We went barefoot all summer and those shells were hard on the feet, periodically bringing *Mr. Bowden* (who was not, as far as I know, a relative) to mind unfavorably. Also, according to *Mr. Murray*, *Mr. Bowden* believed that one got more nourishment by keeping food inside the body as long as possible. That made him well known for the noisy, malodorous flatulence produced as his body relaxed when he fell asleep in church. (I still wonder if *Mr. Bowden* left any good memories behind.)

Two other tales come to mind about rural Delmarva. One was about prisoners escaping from the Georgetown Jail about 16 miles up the Dupont Highway. *Mr. Murray* alleviated the concern that escapees might come south. He said that the only one who had done that had his hand blown off by a shotgun blast when he touched a farmer's screen door. As a result, the escapees all headed north, toward Wilmington and Philadelphia, where they could hide better. The other story was about gypsies who used to come to the area each year, camping in the same field. They left after a few days, well before daybreak. One year a farmer found one of his pigs missing the day the gypsies left, but said nothing about it. The next year, he predicted the gypsies' departure and sat in wait. When the gypsies where ready to leave, one came across the field toward the pigpen, and was felled by a shotgun blast. The other gypsies carried him away. They never came back. As unlikely as these stories seem, they do, in my view, reflect a rural Delmarva attitude prevalent when self-sufficiency was essential.

Mr. Murray brought the young billy goat and wagon to our house for a test run, because his grandson was too little to handle the reins. I became the tester. The surprisingly strong goat immediately bolted, tossing me about six feet and overturning the wagon. *Mr. Murray* stopped the show. But a few months later, that goat was pulling the wagon and grandson with docility evident in every step. The point having been made to the goat and doubting people, we didn't see much more of the goat-drawn wagon.

Mr. Murray told me that the best way to pick a wife is to look for a barefoot young woman working hard in a farm field–because that's how he found *Miss Addie*. Her reply to his provocative comments was always a mild *Now George*, and I can't remember seeing her angry.

I watched my father harness *Mr. Murray's* mule in the barnyard once. When he put the bridle on, the mule pulled backward, bending *Dad* over forward. The goat gave him a very solid butt on his exposed bottom, propelling *Dad* sharply ahead. My father claimed that the mule and goat had deliberately ganged up on him to do that.

Catholics were then relatively rare in southern Delaware. (Georgetown, about 16 miles north, had the nearest Catholic church.) When a Catholic family moved into Millsboro (six miles north), *Mr. Murray* commented: *The Papists air a'comin.* There was no animosity behind the comment, though. The Catholic family was well accepted and the son, a good athlete, was quite popular.

Rural people are often disparaged for their lack of knowledge. But, in their own arena, they're more canny than most outsiders. As *Mr. Murray* said: *City folk don't know nothin' about trading horses.* Another perspective, stated by former Secretary of Defense Donald Rumsfeld, is: *If a person with a rural accent says "I don't know anything about politics," zip your wallet.*

A childhood vignette that often pops into my mind is walking to *Wilmer Lewis'* filling station on Dupont Highway to get a cold soda on a blistering summer day. Several farmers had stopped off there for a cool drink and some joshing. Another one came in while I was drinking my soda. He had a huge family, and was asked how he felt about having so many children. His reply was that he wouldn't take a million dollars for any one of them or give a plugged nickel for airy another. I remember that joviality as representative of the easy camaraderie of people with a common heritage and the ability to find humor and enjoyment in the midst of a short break from oppressive heat and the many years of hard work they had in common.

Another strong memory of our Delmarva neighbors, in town or outside it, is being treated as members of the same community. The men were apt to call me "Little Ebe" even after I grew taller than my father, and felt free to offer me guidance and instruction. *Dad* did nothing to dissuade that, telling me to heed my elders because they were wiser about such things and had my best interests at heart. He was right. They did the best they could for those they saw as their own kind and being part of their own community. There was something to learn from what they said, even (and sometimes especially) when it was wrong.

Religion

Religion came to Delmarva with its settlers, and has been central to individual and community values. The Methodist and Presbyterian religions became predominant.

Directly and indirectly, religion is part of our lives and laws. That's mostly for the good. But, in the case discussed in this section, wrongs on both sides of a religious dispute led to an unpunished killing. The noted Theologian Reinhold Niebuhr made a related observation about human nature:

> *Original sin is that thing about man which makes him capable of*
> *conceiving of his own perfection and incapable of achieving it.*

I first saw a bit about the sect involved when my father took us to see a "Holy Roller" (Pentecostal) service to learn something about our relatives who practiced that religion. We saw a roofed pavilion with open sides and people standing up inside. There was no unusual behavior and we couldn't hear what was being said. *Dad* said getting closer might upset the worshipers, so we left. I now realize that we saw a Christ's Sanctified Holy Church (CSHC) service in or near Omar, Delaware.

CSHC began in the 1880s in the Goodwill Methodist-Episcopal Church of Chincoteague, Virginia.[31] Their minister served several churches. When he held services elsewhere, the charismatic *Joseph B. "Brighter Days Ahead" Lynch* held the services in Chincoteague. *Joseph* had moved from Sussex County, Delaware to Assateague Island, where he was a lighthouse keeper for a time[32] and prospered as the owner of a farm, a store, and several oyster beds.[33]

My ancestral family was involved in CSHC's beginnings. Among these were *William (Billy) Chandler* and his wife *Sarah Elizabeth Benson Chandler*. *William* was the son of *Captain Joshua L. Chandler* and *Catherine Mary Lynch Chandler*, my great-great-grandparents. *Catherine Mary* was *Joseph B. Lynch's* sister.

Joseph Lynch concluded that true salvation required both the forgiveness of sin and sanctification (purification) of the soul by the Holy Spirit. That was a part of the Holiness Movement seeking to return Methodism to its roots.[34] According to Millie Brooke Waite's write-up,[35] he first heard about it from street preachers in Philadelphia in 1887.

In 1887, *Joseph* formed the Sanctified Band, which split from the Methodist Church and formed CSHC in 1892.[36] Its initial members included *John E. Collins* and his wife, *Sarah Elizabeth Tarr Collins*. *Sarah*, known as the first woman pastor on Virginia's Eastern Shore, was sanctified in 1889. In 1893, she and *Joseph B. Lynch* wrote the CSHC "Discipline." It banned marriage between unequals (the holy and unholy) and required dissolution of marriages between sanctified and unsanctified individuals. *Joseph* and *Sarah* established a watch-mate relationship and, after *Joseph* died, his son *Jim Henry Lynch* and *Sarah Collins* had two daughters.[37] (Watch-mate relationships seem to have ranged from a chaste mutual practice of religion to spousal relationships, with the latter being more common.)

Separation from unsanctified spouses was a CSHC teaching, but remaining in the same house with a former spouse was acceptable too. *Joseph Lynch* left his wife Charlotte and made *Sarah Tarr Collins* his watch-mate, but *Sarah* kept her first husband's surname and lived with him, before and after leaving Chincoteague, and after having children by *Jim Henry Lynch*.[38] *William Chandler* also lived with his first wife and their children until having a child with his second spouse.[39] These examples show no overlap in birth dates of children of different spouses, indicating that CSHC practiced serial monogamy, not polygamy or free love. Moreover, all indications are that CSHC's people believed their actions were right in the eyes of God, including, for *Joseph Lynch and Sarah Tarr Collins,* the following relationships.

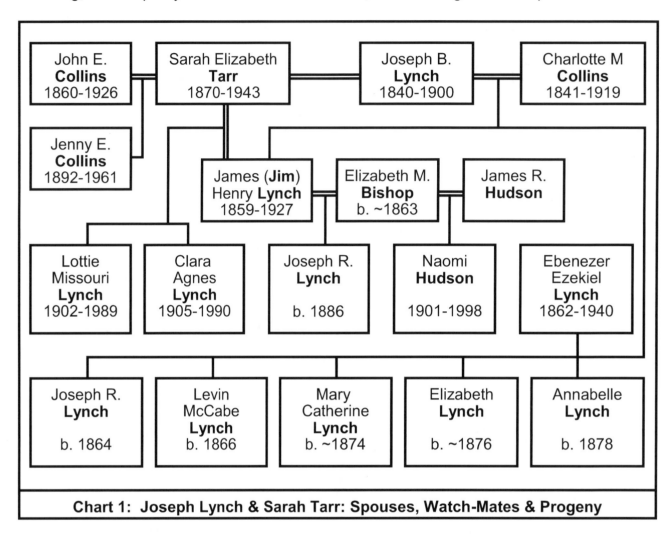

Chart 1: Joseph Lynch & Sarah Tarr: Spouses, Watch-Mates & Progeny

The community initially accepted CSHC, became outraged when its married individuals took new spouses, and then persecuted the sect.[40] *Joseph Lynch* was among those financially ruined[41] by the associated ostracism and boycotting.[42]

On September 1, 1894, 11 young men reportedly out to punish CSHC for immoralities rode noisily up Chincoteague's Main Street toward the CSHC building, which was next to (and bigger than) the Methodist Church. During their return, one of them began shooting. A bullet entered the second floor bedroom of *Captain Aaron Thomas Bowden's* Main Street home, killing him as he lay asleep in bed. A Founding Member of CSHC, *Tom* had ended his affiliation with that church a few weeks earlier.[43] He and his wife, *Mary Catherine (Cassie) Chandler Bowden*, the niece of *Joseph B. Lynch*, had six (maybe seven) young children at the time.[44]

One of the group that killed *Tom Bowden* was known for his dislike of CSHC, and had been fined for assaulting *Joseph Lynch*. All the young men, reputedly, were from the "best" families of Chincoteague and were expressing community sentiment. No one was tried for the killing, which was ruled an accident. CSHC was blamed for the violence.[45] The why behind that is puzzling–until one realizes that convicting the killer(s) also would have morally convicted the community.

CHSC was not itself violent. It did not respond in kind to assaults like the one against *Joseph B Lynch,*[46] or to acts such as the reported burning of their parent church and the one they built in Frankford, Delaware.[47] (The newspaper article describing the burnings also stated[48] that it was thought that *Tom Bowden* was murdered and his wife shot at because they opposed the Sanctified Band.)

About a week after *Tom Bowden's* death, four CSHC members were each charged with four misdemeanors: conspiring to commit indecent acts; causing a wife to leave her husband; conspiring to promulgate free love by teaching wives to disregard their marriage vows; and conspiring to appoint a male and female member as fellow-watchers to sit up at night and watch. The accused did not put up bail and were all jailed. A petition was circulated to ask the court to revoke CSHC preachers' authority to perform marriages. Later newspaper reports stated that, if the courts and the state didn't act, other means would be sought to rid the community of CSHC, and that the citizens felt that CSHC's practices had to be stopped–by force if necessary.[49]

The accused were tried in October 1894. *John Collins* was acquitted. *Joseph B. Lynch* was fined $250 and sentenced to eight months in jail. *William (Billy) Chandler* was fined $150 and sentenced to six months. *Sarah Collins* was fined $100 and sentenced to four months.[50] (Those were severe sentences for misdemeanors. At 3% inflation, $250 in 1895 became over $6000 in 2007.)

The convicted were freed on bail pending appeal. They left town for good, followed by CSHC emigres who sold their property at sacrificial prices. Their four-year-old church, which cost $2000 to build, was auctioned off for $100. CSHC then began evangelical travels, and encountered more hostile treatment.[51] In Chowan, North Carolina, some CSHC members were killed by the gunfire used to drive them out.[52]

CSHC resumed services in Chincoteague in 1903, without repudiating spouses or community animosity[53] (indicating mutual recognition of contribution to the killing).

Joseph B. Lynch died of typhoid fever in Fernandina, Florida in 1900. CSHC stopped repudiating spouses several years later. Its congregations still worship exuberantly. (They still have 15 churches.[54]) In church, they do not wear jewelry or make-up or play musical instruments. Fund-raising events are prohibited, and their ministers are volunteers.[55]

Parents' actions are not their children's fault. So no one alive is to blame for the early actions of CSHC or its detractors.[56] And, only those of us without sin should be throwing stones. But we can learn from the acts of the people involved.

CSHC terminated marriages and established new spousal relationships without regard for man's laws or community mores. They thereby did not "Render unto Caesar...." That tore families apart.[57] CHSC was otherwise troublesome too. They sent out emissaries two by two, as Jesus had. But their "Discipline" asserted that preaching singly was not in accordance with God's word.[58] That was inconsistent with the way Jesus taught and preached[59] and with the Sanctified Band's prior petitioning of the Methodist Bishop to send *a* holy man to preach to them.[60] Also, CSHC's early demeanor was described as more zealous than their Methodist minister could endure.[61] Their actions seem to have been unwise, or self-serving, or inconsistent, or contrary to their basic creed (the Bible), and unduly provocative. That was the first step toward killing *Tom Bowden* (the unlocking of Pandora's Box).

The community responded by endorsing and taking personal actions against CSHC. That was the second step toward the killing (the opening of Pandora's Box).

The third, and worst, wrong was the shooting (the evil coming out of Pandora's Box). That shot was described as being fired into the air.[62] But it seems more likely that the shooter had a short range pistol or derringer (perhaps a smoothbore) and fired it at the house from across, and perhaps up, Main Street. That way, the bullet's apex could have been reached at about the second floor level, with the slowing (falling) bullet entering the house and hitting Tom Bowden in bed. (A bullet fired up into the air from horseback would be coming out of the gun at about 10 feet above the ground and would be entering the house while coming down sharply, relatively spent, and at an angle as least as steep as it went up. It would be more likely to enter through the roof than, as this bullet was described as having entered, through the wall or window. And, the roof and bedroom ceiling impacts would have slowed the bullet even further, making a fatality unlikely.)

Religious differences often are accompanied by long-lasting persecution and killing. (See Appendix 2.) The wrongs in CSHC's early acts and Chincoteague's response were minimal by comparison, and Chincoteague's residents were less violent than the shooters in Chowan, North Carolina. But that wouldn't have consoled *Tom Bowden's* immediate survivors–it's hard to find good in the killing of a loved one.

It further seems fair to note that, in the USA at least, a killing like *Tom Bowden's* could, today, have severe civil and criminal consequences.

CSHC believed that forgiveness of sins and Sanctification produces sinlessness. They even appear to have believed that they could do no wrong. But, once they recognized that harm was occurring, they ceased the associated practices. One result has been widespread recognition (for close to 100 years now) that their congregations are good and responsible citizens.[63]

CSHC's early actions and the reactions of others (both of which we are all inherently capable) are a lesser example of the trait stated by noted French Mathematician and Philosopher Blaise Pascal as:

> ***Men never do evil so completely and cheerfully as when they do it from religious conviction.***

Chandler Family Ancestors

Hereditary surnames in Britain developed in the 13th and 14th centuries. They were used in census-like records. The Chandler surname originated from "candela," the Latin name for candle. It came to mean candle-maker.[64] Candle-makers began making soap and selling it and other items to ships, and "chandler" became the occupational name for such suppliers. When the British Poll Tax[65] (a head tax) arrived in the late 1300s, a lot of unrelated chandlers took the Chandler surname. So far, Chandler family DNA testing has confirmed that wide genetic base.[66]

Chandler surname variations include: Chandeler, Chandlers, Chandlor, Chanler, Channdler, Channdlers, Chantler, Chaundeler, Chaundler, Chaundlor, etc.

- Delmarva's Chandler family has roots in Sussex County, Delaware and Chincoteague, Virginia. So far, knowledge of my Chandler ancestors begins with Captain Joshua L. Chandler (1829-1877). Except for his father's name and his mother's forename, Captain Joshua's ancestors haven't been identified. Potential ancestors[67] include:

- John Chandler, who arrived at Jamestown, Virginia on June 10, 1610 on the "Hercules" as part of a three ship expedition led by Lord Delaware, Sir Thomas West of Hampshire. U.S. descendants of Robert Chandler, believed to be a younger son of John, number in the thousands.

- John Chandler (c.1648-1728) of Accomack County, Virginia. He and his wife Margaret appear in county records until early 1728.

- George Chandler, a 1686 Wilshire emigre who died on the voyage. His widow Jane and their seven or eight children settled in Delaware (then the lower three counties of Pennsylvania). DNA testing shows George to be related to John Chandler of Jamestown and to other Chandlers of Hampshire.

- John Chandler (c.1685-1735), a land owner in/near Port Tobacco in Charles County, Maryland. (The Port Tobacco River empties into the east side of the Potomac River, which empties into the west side of the Chesapeake Bay.)

Some Chandlers *may* have emigrated to Ireland in the 17th Century, among the "Cromwellian Adventurers for Land."[68] But, Hampshire is on England's south coast, with Wiltshire immediately inland to its northwest, and the family linkage to that area makes it seem unlikely that Delmarva's Chandlers came from Ireland.

So far, no Delmarva Chandler family male DNA data is available to show ancestral information.

Captain Joshua L. Chandler (1829-1877)

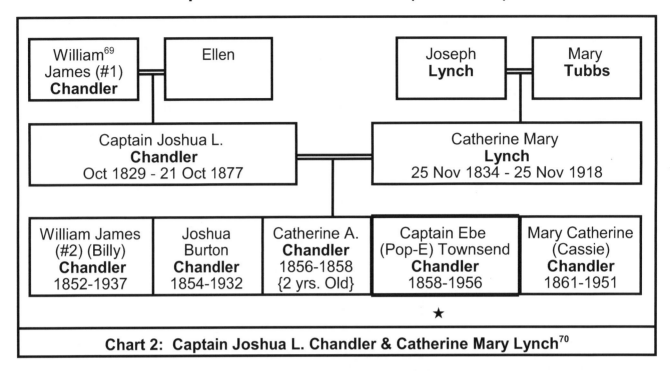

Chart 2: Captain Joshua L. Chandler & Catherine Mary Lynch[70]

Like many of his contemporaries, *Captain Joshua* could not read or write. He and his brother *William James (#3) Chandler, Jr.* (about whom nothing else is known[71]), were born in Roxana, Sussex County, Delaware. After marrying, *Joshua* lived nearby, at Sandy Landing. His son *Billy* was born in Pennsylvania, his other children in Sussex County. And there they lost little *Catherine Ann(a)*. Childhood death rates were higher in early America than is the case today, but their severe impact hasn't changed. Dwight D. Eisenhower expressed that well when he stated about his first son's death:

> ***There's no tragedy in life like the death of a child.***
> ***Things never get back to the way they were.***

In the Civil War, *Joshua L. Chandler* was a Union Army private in Company D, 6th Regiment, Delaware Infantry for a short time. Sometime after the 1870 census, he moved to Chincoteague, Virginia, where he captained a schooner and an oyster dredge. *Captain Joshua* was killed by lightning in 1877, while afloat in a schooner with his sons *Joshua B* and *Ebe* in Cat's Creek off Wallop's Island. *Joshua B.* poled their dismasted craft the 2-3 miles back to Chincoteague. *Ebe* carried their father's body ashore.[72] The Captain was entombed in a coffin-sized, aboveground marble crypt at the North end of town. That's now the Chandler Cemetery, with one marked grave.[73] The epitaph on the tomb is:

> **Farewell wife and children dear**
> **I am not dead but sleeping here**
> **As I am someday you will be**
> **Prepare for death and follow me**

William James Chandler (1852-1937)

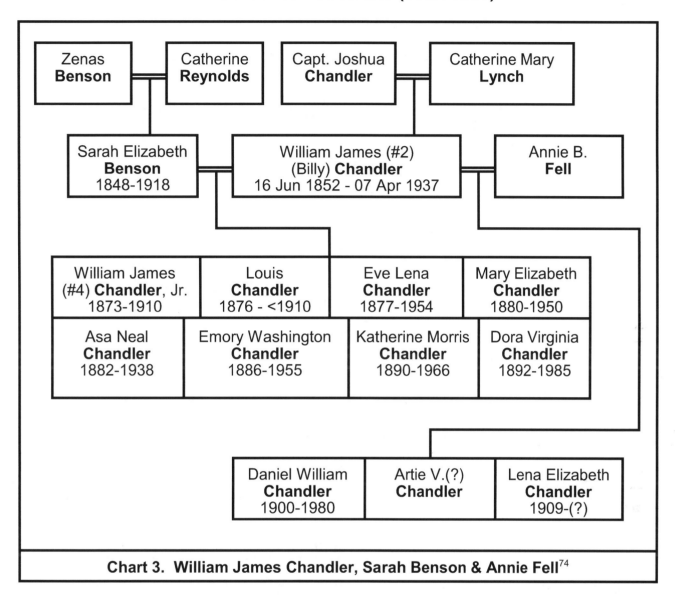

Chart 3. William James Chandler, Sarah Benson & Annie Fell[74]

Great-Grand-Uncle Billy was born so tiny that it was said he could be fit into a quart jar. He survived against the odds, grew into a feisty and proficient scrapper,[75] and became an influential member of Christ's Sanctified Holy Church (CSHC). He and *Sarah* had eight children before CSHC was formed. *Uncle Billy* left Chincoteague in 1984. *Sarah* and their children, except *William Jr.*, followed, living with him until 1900, when he began living with his second spouse. *Sarah* apparently remained a CSHC member, traveled with her church, and showed no ill will toward *Billy*.

Billy Chandler lived in Alabama, Florida, Georgia, Mississippi, North Carolina, Oklahoma, South Carolina, and Virginia. He worked as a carpenter and as a steamship captain. *Sarah,* his first spouse*,* died at a camp meeting in Kansas City, Kansas. Her daughter *Mary Elizabeth* is buried in the CSHC Campgrounds in Perry, Georgia. So is *Annie Fell*, his second spouse. *Uncle Billy,* who was respected in his church and beloved by his family, died and was buried in Wilmington, North Carolina.

Joshua Burton Chandler (1854-1942)

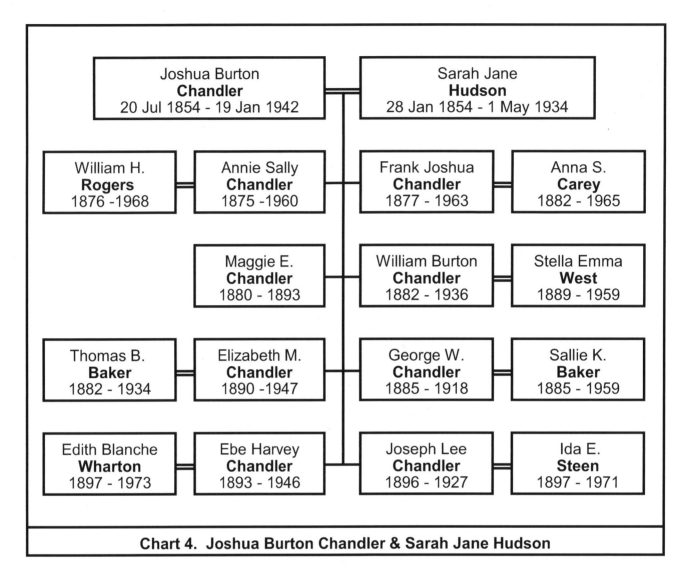

Joshua Burton Chandler 20 Jul 1854 - 19 Jan 1942	**Sarah Jane Hudson** 28 Jan 1854 - 1 May 1934

William H. Rogers 1876 -1968 — **Annie Sally Chandler** 1875 -1960

Frank Joshua Chandler 1877 - 1963 — **Anna S. Carey** 1882 - 1965

Maggie E. Chandler 1880 - 1893

William Burton Chandler 1882 - 1936 — **Stella Emma West** 1889 - 1959

Thomas B. Baker 1882 - 1934 — **Elizabeth M. Chandler** 1890 -1947

George W. Chandler 1885 - 1918 — **Sallie K. Baker** 1885 - 1959

Edith Blanche Wharton 1897 - 1973 — **Ebe Harvey Chandler** 1893 - 1946

Joseph Lee Chandler 1896 - 1927 — **Ida E. Steen** 1897 - 1971

Chart 4. Joshua Burton Chandler & Sarah Jane Hudson

Joshua Burton Chandler settled in Dagsboro, Sussex County, Delaware as a retail merchant and farmer. His father, *Captain Joshua Chandler*, and then his 53-year-old son, *William Burton Chandler,* both died on the water–his father from lightning, his son from drowning. *William*, the largest fruit broker on the Eastern Shore and an Anne Arundel Academy graduate, went crabbing in the Indian River and didn't come home. His boat was found adrift. The river was dragged during the night. About 6 am, his body was found, standing a few inches below the surface in a half-drooped position, with his hands showing signs of a struggle to hold onto the boat.

Joshua Burton's son *Ebe Harvey Chandler* met his wife *Blanche* at Sandy Landing, where he and one of his brothers were selling ice cream on a stick at two for a nickel, using the cry: Hokey Pokeys, Two for Five; Stick 'em in ya, Dead or Alive. *Ebe Harvey* and his brother *Joseph* had a garage in Dagsboro for four years–until *Ebe Harvey* was appointed Dagsboro's Postmaster by President Harding. Initially elected to the State Senate in 1935, *Ebe Harvey* was the Republican Floor Leader there from 1936-37. (*Blanche* served as postmistress while he was a State Senator.) He also served as State Motor Vehicle Commissioner and on the

Unemployment Compensation Commission and, with *William "Buff" McCabe,* owned the Chandler and McCabe Feed Store in Dagsboro. In addition, *Ebe Harvey* was the Delco and Frigidaire District Manager for Delaware, Maryland and Pennsylvania, and owned Burton's Island, where he had a boathouse and racing speedboats. His son *Hilton* never developed beyond infantile responses and was tended to as an infant, by his grandmother, until he died at age 17. His daughter Reba died at age 12 in a truck accident. In 1946, at the age of 53, *Ebe Harvey* died instantaneously in a head-on car crash. His family is shown below.

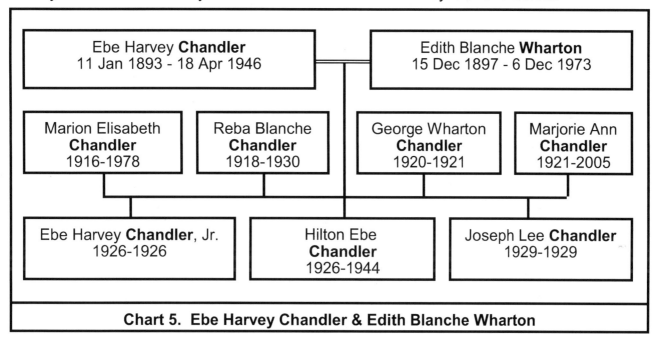

Chart 5. Ebe Harvey Chandler & Edith Blanche Wharton

Blanche Wharton Chandler buried her husband and five of her seven children before reaching her 49th birthday. She was nonetheless a positive and upbeat influence on her surviving descendants. That makes her heroic, at least by the criterion of the famous Chemist and Microbiologist Louis Pasteur, who stated: *It is surmounting difficulties that makes heroes.*

There are lighter notes here too. When 24-year-old *Marion Elisabeth Chandler* eloped with 25-year-old *Harry "Pete" Hancock,* they returned to their parents' homes for three days, while they worked up the nerve to tell *Marion's* father.

In 1948, *Pete Hancock* and *Alvin "Skeet" Campbell, Marjorie Ann Chandler's* husband, built Dagsboro's Clayton Theater. Whether Sunday night movies would lure people away from church became an issue. The movies were scheduled after church, the naysayers' dispersed, and the community enjoyed the theater.

Cassandra (Sandie) Gerken is the daughter of *Pete* and *Marion Hancock.* Her meticulous research, and that of her sister, *Jane McComrick,* is a cornerstone of the genealogy of the Eastern Shore Chandlers.

Mary Catherine Chandler (1861-1951)

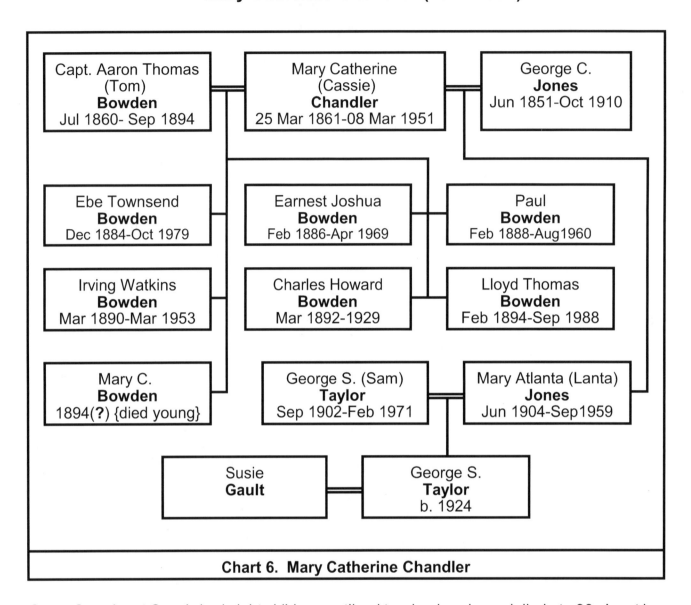

Chart 6. Mary Catherine Chandler

Great-Grandaunt Cassie had eight children, outlived two husbands, and died at ~90. I met her when she was living with *Sam and Lanta Taylor* in Chincoteague. While my parents and great-grandfather visited, *Granduncle Sam* let my brother and me pole his flat-bottomed scow about the shallows. (He used it to get to and from his charter fishing boat.) Then he gave us a brick, a hammer, and a bushel of delicious clams to enjoy. I remember the kindly *Taylors*, and only faintly recall *Aunt Cassie*–and her frailty. But hers was a weakness of age and not of character. When her first husband was killed, *Aunt Cassie* was 33 years old and had six (perhaps seven) young children living. The oldest was about 10, the youngest less than a year. *Aunt Cassie* was then a single head of household for four years–in a world in which women were strongly relegated to the role of homemaker.

Captain Ebe Townsend Chandler (1858-1956)

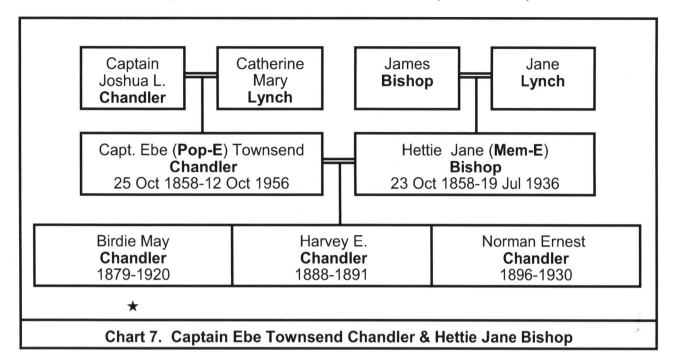

Chart 7. Captain Ebe Townsend Chandler & Hettie Jane Bishop

Captain Ebe T. Chandler was born in Roxana, Sussex County, Delaware. The origin of his forename may be Eber, the name of the oldest son of the chief of the mythical Parthalonian settlers of Ireland,[76] or it may be Ebenezer, an Old Testament word meaning "Stone of Help."[77] In any case, the name has a long history in rural Delmarva: *Josiah Campbell*, born in 1810 in Sussex County, had an older brother named *Ebe*.[78]

Ebe T. Chandler wed *Hettie Jane Bishop* when they were both 18. They settled in Sussex County in Frankford. Their first child was stillborn. The second, *Birdie,* died at age 42. *Harvey*, the next, died at age three. The fourth, *Norman*, was killed at age 34. *Pop-E* and *Mem-E* had the misfortune to outlive all their children, and *Pop-E* outlived *Mem-E* by 20 years.

My father, the first grandchild, couldn't say Pop-Pop-Ebe or Mom-Mom-Hettie. So they became *Pop-E* and *Mem-E* to the whole family. (That was *Mem-E's* second renaming. *Pop-E* called her *Hattie*, and put that name on her tombstone.)

After his father died, *Pop-E* helped out his mother and his sister *Cassie,* and later loaned *Cassie* the money to buy a home. He put his grandson *Harley* through college and law school. *Pop-E* brought his *Step-Grandfather Sharp* to live with him and *Mem-E* in their Frankford home, and buried him in his (*Pop-E's*) own plot in Carey Cemetery in Frankford. Also, according to my father, *Pop-E* pushed Frankford into getting electric street lights, loaning the town the money for them. I never heard him speak about his generosity. That was family lore.

Pop-E had only one year of school. He first went to sea as a cabin boy (reportedly at age 12), taught himself reading, writing and navigation, became a cook, and studied for his master's license. About 25 candidates took the exam. *Pop-E* and one other passed. But no one was ready to make a cook a Captain. Then *Pop-E's* Captain was lost at sea in a storm and his having the only master's license aboard made him Captain for the rest of that voyage. Impressed with the ship being brought safely through, the owner gave *Pop-E* the job.

Pop-E contracted double pneumonia when his three-year-old, 358 ton oceangoing tug, the Spartan,[79] sank about six nautical miles northwest of Cape Henlopen, Delaware on September 16, 1903, during the Vagabond Hurricane. *Pop-E* was rescued 13 hours later, still clinging to a 13' X 4" wood scantling.[80] (His rescuer was a seaman *Pop-E* had rescued the previous year.) *Pop-E* wasn't expected to live but recovered undaunted. (The hurricane's 80 mph winds also caused the yacht President Theodore Roosevelt was aboard off Long Island to hasten into port, and killed 30 people in a shipwreck off Chincoteague, Virginia.[81])

I doubt that *Pop-E* ever weighed as much as 140 pounds. But, he was huge in presence, courage, feistiness, and physical skill–and was very, very quick in movement as well as temper. One story about his exploits was about stevedores on strike in Philadelphia refusing to unload his ship. *Pop-E* took umbrage and went down the pier, knocking the strikers into the water one by one. Like many tales about *Pop-E*, this one is far-fetched, but it is consistent with his nature.

My father said *Pop-E* made his fortune in ship salvage, putting to sea in storms that kept other captains in port. *Dad* described going to sea with *Pop-E* as including charging ahead through dense fog. He even thought *Pop-E* could tell where other ships were by hearing their foghorns. (That's not possible.) But *Pop-E* was steeped in seagoing lore. So his willingness to take risks may have been mitigated by a deeper sense of the sea than that of his competitors.

At sea, *Pop-E* wore shirts with detachable collars, and took off his tie and collar before going to bed. Then he removed his shoes, putting them next to the bed with the toes facing out. Next came his pants, laid out so he could put his stockinged feet through them and directly into his shoes. When awakened about a problem, he sat up, put his feet into his shoes, stood up, pulled up his pants, buckled his belt, and was on deck to handle things in less than a minute.

Spiritualism was part of *Pop-E's* life. He talked about his first experience with it being a seance in Florida and being told that the spirits would contact him, with that happening as predicted. Further, he described being told by the spirits about a death at sea, and about then telling the man's wife that her husband had been lost, and how, and about the confirmation coming months later. My father said that really happened.

Pop-E was a faith healer until iodized salt eliminated goiters (his specialty). Once, when *Dad* visited while feeling ill, *Pop-E* had him sit down, rubbed his hands along *Dad's* spine, and asked him if he felt anything. *Dad* said he didn't, and *Pop-E* concluded that his powers were gone. *Mom* also asked if *Dad* had felt anything. He said that he had felt a powerful sensation under *Pop-E's* fingers, and denied it because he thought *Pop-E* might take up faith healing again.

Every winter, *Pop-E* drove himself to the Plant City Hotel in Tampa, Florida. He often remarked that he had stayed there for 30 years at the same rate. (His holding the hotel mortgage may have been a factor.) That ended when *Pop-E* was 92 and made it to the Carolinas before phoning my father to come and drive him back home. *Dad* took the next bus out.

Pop-E bought some Florida orange groves and had to sell at a huge loss when seedless oranges took over the market. *Dad* said that the groves included several acres that became part of Tampa. If that's true, *Pop-E* took two major losses on the venture. That didn't impoverish him, but did limit his generosity. Also, his orange grove adventure illustrates the often overlooked reality that success demands comprehensive knowledge and experience.

Aunt Virginia considered *Pop-E* a mixed blessing. He cared deeply, but his hot temper, demanding nature and strict discipline were difficult. One of his favorite statements was: *I am Captain of this ship, from stem to stern*. The ship, of course, was wherever he happened to be.

Aunt Virginia heard that statement a lot when she was growing up. And, she once described overhearing *Pop-E* tell *Mem-E* that *Virginia* was just like *Birdie*, with *Mem-E* vigorously disagreeing by stating that *Birdie* had minded her, but *Virginia* didn't.

Aunt Virginia often spoke about the exceptional dancing skill that *Pop-E* showed on the dance floor on the second floor of Wilgus' Bowling Alley in Bethany Beach, Delaware. He was a much sought after dance partner, and taught *Aunt Virginia* the Charleston. She too became very skilled, and was offered a job with a touring dance group. *Pop-E* summarily rejected that offer.

Pop-E spoke about his age in an unusual way: when he was 86, he would say he was in his 87th year. *Dad* explained that a birth day is not a birthday: we are born zero years old but in our first year. Dates are stated like that (2010 is in the 21st Century), but *Pop-E* is the only person I've heard express age like that.

Never having had an automobile accident was a matter of pride to *Pop-E*. But he had a permanently crooked finger. My father, after much prodding, explained why. *Pop-E* bought his first car, drove it home (another first), had his family pack, and drove them to Boston. He drove off a "cliff" there and injured his finger. (I've often wondered what that entire journey was like.)

Pop-E avowed that he had never been late or drunk. I never knew him to be either. But he did use Courvoisier VSOP brandy as medicine and once asked *Aunt Virginia* to get him some. She asked *Dad* to do it because ladies do not go into liquor stores. He took over the task.

Pop-E often said that he and *Mem-E* never had a cross word. But *Mom* said his fondness for the ladies caused heated arguments with *Mem-E*. And, he had a long-term association with *"Aunt Kate,"* *Mem-E's* niece. In *Pop-E's* later years, she still spent part of her summers with him. I thought that no one questioned *Pop-E* about anything. But *Aunt Virginia* asked him about other women, and was told that we can control a lot of things but not our hearts.

The *Aunt Kate* situation (whatever it was) notwithstanding, *Pop-E* did not endorse misbehavior. An example was the lifestyle of his grandson *Harley*, who liked luxury. During his occasional visits from Detroit, he would have preferred staying at *Pop-E's* house. But, when he visited as a bachelor, accompanied by an attractive, unmarried lady, they stayed with us and slept on a very uncomfortable sofa bed in our cramped farmhouse, with no indoor bathroom. (*Mom*, after they left, gave *Dad* holy hell about the stay–in a very one-sided discussion.) When *Uncle Harley* finally did marry, and visited, he stayed with *Pop-E*. Being married made the difference. My mother's and *Mem-E's* concerns may have been overly puritanical, and *Pop-E's* popularity as a dancer may have caused some unjustified concern, and there may have been some fire under the smoke. But *Pop-E* was not, by nature, a philanderer or an enabler of marital misbehavior.

Mom sometimes spoke disapprovingly of *Pop-E's* fondness for the opposite sex with a smiling, head-shaking admiration. An example was her description of him in a hospital bed in a corridor before a room was assigned. She said she knew he was going to be OK when an attractive nurse passed by. *Pop-E* raised his head to look and weakly commented: *Ain't bad, is she?*

When I was two and we were staying with *Pop-E* while he was ill, the foyer stairway was barricaded so I couldn't get hurt on it. But I broke through and was found upstairs visiting my delighted great-grandfather.

Mom never complained about the workload *Pop-E's* illnesses brought. She once nursed him for about six months in Philadelphia, while he recovered from prostate removal surgery. That was probably before she and *Dad* started a family.

Pop-E once asked me what I was reading. It was an article describing an old-time boxer as better than he had been perceived. *Pop-E* read some of it and said that the man wasn't all that much and he had beaten him himself, in Stillman's Gym. I believed him. (*Dad* said that *Pop-E* was a trained and very proficient fighter.)

Pop-E told me that, if a fight was coming, to get in the first blow, making it a good one. Not long afterwards, at grade school recess, a boy about my size was pushing my younger brother around. I told him to stop. He blustered. I drew a line in the dirt with my shoe and dared him to step across. As he did, I punched him in the face as hard as I could. He went flat on his back, still blustering but not getting up. We had no more trouble with him.

In his eighties, *Pop-E* was stopped for speeding by an about 6'2", 220 pound State Trooper. He chased the officer, uttering his favorite imprecations: *You can't fan a fly off of me; I can whip you faster than Hell can scorch a feather!* The trooper retreated to his cruiser and drove off. No ticket was issued. (I think the matter was handled through my father.)

Mem-E died when I was about three. My only remembrance of her is a story about her tapioca pudding. *Mom* told her that I wouldn't eat it. But *Mem-E* fed it to me and I gobbled it down. Mom never forgot that I ate something from *Mem-E's* hand that I wouldn't touch from hers.

My memory of *Pop-E* begins with a trip from New York City to spend a vacation with him. That involved a train ride from Pennsylvania Station to Harrington, Delaware, and then a bus trip to Bethany Beach. *Mom* dressed my brother and me in sparkling white shirts, shorts, knee-length socks, and shoes. The trip was long and the anticipation high. When we arrived, I eagerly leapt out–into viscous, waist-deep, coal-black muck in the roadside ditch. I've never forgotten that. Neither did *Mom*. But neither *Pop-E* nor my father ever mentioned it to me.

When I knew him, *Pop-E* lived in the house he bought for his daughter in Frankford so she wouldn't have to live in the same building as the Post Office and General Store. She died a few years later, and *Pop-E* moved there to bring up his granddaughter *Virginia*. He then had the house moved back and raised onto blocks, put an open porch on three sides, and added cupolas with stained glass windows on the front porch corners. The porch across the back was walled in, and part of it became the kitchen. The home is now a registered national historic site.

As a boy I found *Pop-E's* house awesome, especially the grandfather's clock in the foyer, the Tiffany lamp producing a warm light around it, and the sailing ship model in a glass case in the parlor. *Pop-E's* bedroom was on the front of the second floor. The bathroom was in the back of that floor, with the toilet next to a tall, low-bottomed window. One had to pull down the window shade before using the toilet, and raise the shade afterwards. *Dad* evaded my questions about that for many years. He finally explained that it was the first flush toilet in Frankford. (The former, four-seat outhouse is still in the back yard.) *Pop-E* had the window installed because he wanted the town to know about indoor plumbing.

My brother and I played with an old tricycle with high handlebars and no seat at *Pop-E's* house. A treadle between its wheels propelled it rapidly. But the old toy couldn't withstand our exuberance and collapsed. We abashedly told our parents, very much aware that *Pop-E* had kept the tricycle because it had been his children's toy. But he only said that he was glad we had enjoyed it. (During a college engineering course, I concluded that the tricycle's propulsion mechanism resembled the planetary gear train termed an Irish Mail, that the toy was rare and perhaps unique, and that it would be a museum piece if we hadn't demolished it.)

During *Pop-E's* periodic illnesses, we moved in with him so *Mom* could provide nursing care. My brother and I then slept in a large, third floor bedroom. It was very cold there in winter, but we kept warm by having a feather mattress beneath us and another one as a quilt. Being up there in the dark was scary. When the steam engine train passed through Frankford about 3:00 a.m. every morning, its eerie whistle awakened me. After silence returned, I strained to hear any noises that could be attributed to spirits. But I never heard anything but the comforting gong and chimes of the grandfather's clock.

During a stay with *Pop-E* while he was sick when I was about 10, autumn leaves were falling. He insisted that they be removed. I was tasked with raking up and burning them, and making sure the fire didn't spread. When *Pop-E* looked out the window, he saw that I was burning the leaves in the middle of the side lawn. My initial awareness of his displeasure was an enraged bellow coming from him as he stood on the porch in his nightshirt and cap. There was a long, swinging gate at the back of the yard. It was about my height, taller than the wrought iron fence along the street, but it had a smooth top. I fled over it. When I came back a few hours later, the leaves were gone. After supper, my father quietly explained how I should have done the job.

Pop-E paid a lot of attention to that lawn. It was cut with a push mower, using half the swath so each spot received a double going over. The mowing process was to take three steps forward and two steps back. Meticulous supervision caused *Pop-E* to run out of help. My father volunteered me and I reported for duty with all the apprehension of a child facing a volcanic taskmaster. *Pop-E* carefully gave me my instructions, stood on the porch in one of the dark blue three-piece suits he typically wore, and coached the mowing—repeatedly reminding me to use no more than half the mower's width. (It soon became obvious that the mowing wasn't uniform because the steps back were shorter and fewer than the steps forward, but I kept that to myself.) After mowing, I pulled up everything that dared to grow under the wrought iron fence, and put salt down as a growth deterrent. It all took about six hours. *Pop-E* pronounced the mowing the best the lawn had ever had, said the job was mine and he was going to pay me the same as the grown men who had preceded me, and gave me a shiny 50¢ piece. I thanked him, got on the bike my brother and I shared, and wearily pedaled home.

Dad asked me about the mowing. I said I wasn't going to do it again because it was too hard and fifty cents was too little. He said that, if my great-grandfather wanted me to mow his lawn, I would do it whether he paid me or not. So mow it I did—getting a very shiny half-dollar coin every time—*Pop-E* was a man of his word. I later discovered from my father's attitude and then from my own that we tend to treat money as if has the same value as it did when we were young, and 50¢ was a lot more cash when and where *Pop-E* learned the value of a dollar.

In the 1930s, *Pop-E* served eight years as mayor of Bethany Beach. He was also a town commissioner there, and pushed to have the first boardwalk installed. It was laid directly onto the sand in Spring and taken up in Winter.

In Delaware, *Pop-E* drove us to Bethany Beach on summer Sundays and strolled the boardwalk in a summer suit and Panama hat while we played in the water. The trip was made in his big, black 1938 Hudson sedan. (The hot ride, with the windows rolled down for cooling, and the whumping noise encountered when we came abreast of a car headed in the other direction on the two-lane road remain a very clear memory.) As he aged, *Pop-E's* driving made the trip more adventuresome, but not enough of a concern to forgo it. At the time, his cottage was still there, next to the boardwalk, a block north of the main access road. *Pop-E* had sold it to a relative with the understanding that the cottage be kept in the family. But it was sold to someone unrelated, reputedly at a 100% profit, a few years later. (The property is now reportedly worth about seven million dollars, so the buyer may have sacrificed a huge long term gain for a windfall.)

A strong memory of that three-story beach "cottage" is its basement with nine shower stalls. No one was allowed to go from the beach to the house without showering. The aura of the house is a distinctive memory, but the cottage went to sea in a storm. Six adjoining two-story condominiums sit where it did.

Pop-E told us about putting jetties in to expand and stabilize the beach, and about the importance of the sand-retaining fences. The jetties are now partly rip-rap and much shorter, the fences are less evident, construction has eliminated a lot of the dunes, erosion has substantially narrowed the beach, and heavy rains now cause flooding along the Beach Highway. Moreover, normal summer traffic jams the roads, the Labor Day exodus is a nightmare, and the summer population is still increasing. So the beach we enjoyed so much gets more dangerous every year.

In thinking about *Pop-E*, I've tried to heed Mark Twain's statement that:

> **To arrive at a just assessment of a renowned man's character one must judge it by the standards of his time, not ours.**

To me, *Pop-E* is still a man of renown. Ship's captains were more important in his day. (Today's ships, weather forecasts, communications, and rescue capabilities are much improved.) Also, temperaments like *Pop-E's* were more prevalent then. An example was President Andrew Jackson (See Appendix 3). Further, the heros of *Pop-E's* early life were Civil War veterans–followed by very tough men like Theodore Roosevelt of Rough Rider fame.

Two William Shakespeare quotes come to mind when I think of *Pop-E*. The first (from *Julius Caesar*) I'll state something like the way my father used to say it:

> **A coward dies a thousand deaths, a brave man only one.**

The second quote (from *Hamlet*) is:

> **There are more things in heaven and earth, Horatio, than are dreamt of in your philosophy.**

Pop-E lived dangerously and tenaciously, and died two weeks before entering his 99th year. Being more skeptical could have been helpful to him, at least financially. But he started with nothing, achieved, surmounted tragedy, and was nurturing, caring and giving. He held no grudges, didn't take people to task for past misdeeds, didn't preach, and complimented good behavior. When he talked to me, he expressed himself in a direct and matter-of-fact way. His striving for perfection and focus on winning are still shining examples (if one realizes that some successes are worse than failure). Like many leaders, especially military ones, he didn't apologize for his faults or mistakes. Overall, I benefitted greatly from knowing him.

Norman Ernest Chandler (1896-1930)

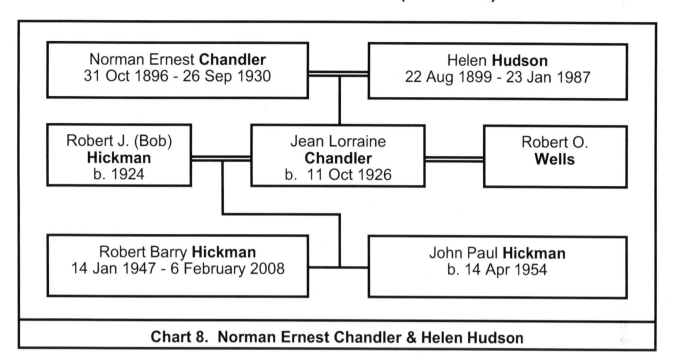

Norman Ernest Chandler 31 Oct 1896 - 26 Sep 1930	**Helen Hudson** 22 Aug 1899 - 23 Jan 1987

| Robert J. (Bob) **Hickman** b. 1924 | Jean Lorraine **Chandler** b. 11 Oct 1926 | Robert O. **Wells** |

| Robert Barry **Hickman** 14 Jan 1947 - 6 February 2008 | John Paul **Hickman** b. 14 Apr 1954 |

Chart 8. Norman Ernest Chandler & Helen Hudson

Granduncle Norman was born 18 years after his sister. As a boy, my father spent a lot of time with his *Uncle Norman* at Bethany Beach. *Pop-E* ruled there with an iron hand, ringing the dinner bell when a meal was ready. Anyone who didn't come promptly had their plate turned over and couldn't eat–because *Mem-E* was not there to provide meals at everyone's convenience. The boys were often late, and *Mem-E* put food aside to sneak to them later. (I'm sure *Pop-E* knew that. A ship's cook learns to keep a close watch on food consumption.)

Dad and his *Uncle Norman* once rode from Wilmington, Delaware to Frankford on a new motorcycle, ruining the bike on that ~100 mile trip on the rough roads of the time. They also sank *Pop-E's* motorboat, while racing it, when its flat bottom caved in from the pounding. Saying they were ahead at the time pacified *Pop-E.*

Granduncle Norman's very attractive and personable daughter *Jean* was six when her father died in a car accident. He tail-ended a wagon carrying a large pole, which came through the windshield and crushed most of his face. *Pop-E* feared that his son hadn't had the time to pray for forgiveness. A pastor's assurance that God grants everyone time to do that comforted him considerably.

Bob, Jean's first husband, was a tail gunner on a WWII B-17 Flying Fortress. After the war, he was attracted to *Jean*, who rejected his attentions. *Bob* sat on her front doorstep for days, until she finally started dating him. I often baby-sat for *Bob* and *Jean* when *Barry* was an infant. Then I went to college, and learned about her second son, her divorce, and her remarriage long afterwards.

My McCabe Family

McCabe name variants include: Abbee, Abee, Cabe, Caybe, MacAbbe, MacAbe, McAbe, M'Caybba (a rare, highland name[82]), McCaybe, McCabee, McCabbee, McKape, and Mecabe. The name's source has been described as: "Scottish and Irish (Cavan): Anglicized form of Gaelic Mac Cába 'son of Cába', a nickname or personal name of uncertain origin."[83] That's consistent with the observation by the McCabe Family DNA Project Coordinator that the McCabe Family DNA Project data shows no common ancestor in historic times between McCabes of different large haplogroups (common DNA sequences).[84] So the five known McCabe DNA haplogroups are not closely related to each other.[85]

The direct line male descendants of *John McCabe (1727-1800)* of lower Sussex County, Delaware bear the Irish Modal Haplotype (DNA sequence) named after Ireland's High King Niall of the Nine Hostages (~342-405),[86] who ruled from 379 AD[87] until his death. Their Uí Néil (now O'Neill) clan genetic signature originated in northern Ireland, where it is most frequent,[88] but Scotland's high incidence of that DNA sequence[89] shows that the Uí Néil also emigrated to Scotland.

Irish surnames became widespread in the 10th Century AD, about 500 years after High King Niall's reign. The estimated two to three million men descended from High King Niall include ones with the Irish surnames O'Neill, (O')Gallagher, Boyle, O'Doherty, O'Conner, Cannon, Bradley, O'Reilly, Flynn, (Mc)Kee, Devlin, Donnelly, Egan, Gormley, Hynes, McCaul, McGovern, McGloughlin, McManus, McMenamin, Molloy, O'Kane, O'Rourke, and Quinn.[90] Descent from Niall is also claimed by the Scottish Clans MacNeil and MacLachlan.[91] Further, because High King Niall lived considerably before surname use became widespread, descent from Niall can be the case with individuals bearing many other surnames.

"Mac Aba," meaning "Son of the Abbott," is a source of the McCabe surname.[92] Abbotts headed monasteries and were supposedly celibate, but some of them may nonetheless have sired some Mac Abas. The surname also may have arisen from instances of the Aba nickname being applied as a surname based on the demeanor of individuals who were religious but not clergymen.

The first known use of Mac Aba was on the Isle of Arran as a sept (subset) of the Scottish Clan MacLeod.[93] (I sailed past Arran over 20 times on a fleet ballistic missile submarine. It looked very vacant, green and chilly.) But the name first came to Ireland from the Hebrides, Scotland's outer islands, not Arran. It was noted as a name occurring on Lewis, a Hebridean Isle occupied by the MacLeod Clan,[94] and is likely to have come from there. (Its incidence wasn't so noted for Harris, the other Macleod-occupied Hebridean Isle.)

Scottish ancestry includes Norse Vikings who settled in the Hebrides,[95] English Celts, Picts, and the Irish Dál Riata Clan from Scotia (northeastern ancient Ireland).[96] The Dál Riata influx began in the late 5th Century AD.[97] It developed into the Dalriadan Kingdom that, beginning about 840 AD,[98] united the Picts and the Irish raiders named Scoti[99] by the Romans into the Kingdom of Scotland.

A second source of McCabe is "Mac Cabe," from the Irish Gaelic term for "Son of the Helmeted One."[100] When the Gaelic Irish started importing Hebridean mercenary gallowglasses[101] to help them regain control[102] of the country after the Anglo-Normans invaded it in 1169, unrelated gallowglasses may have taken the name upon then settling in Ireland. Mac Abes were in the armies of the O'Reillys and O'Rourkes around 1350, in Counties Cavan and Monaghan,[103] just south of what became Protestant "Northern Ireland" (Ulster).

The Irish Scoti included High King Niall who, according to legend, was the captor of a youth born in Roman Britain of English parents.[104] The youth, then named Succat, escaped from Ireland and returned years later to become Ireland's Saint Patrick.[105]

In fecundity, High King Niall is second to Genghis Khan, who has 16 million male descendants.[106] More significant, Scots descended from Niall have direct ancestors who were Irish in Ireland before Saint Patrick converted the country to Christianity.

There was a second large Scottish immigration into Ireland from 1603-1697.[107] When Scotland's King James VI became England's King James I, he established a "Plantation" in Ulster, giving preference in land proprietorship to the Protestant English and Scots. The newcomers were mostly Lowland Scots[108] who brought the Presbyterian religion with them,[109] and immigrated to get better land on easier terms. The Irish met them violently. Combat, farming and organization skills enabled the newcomers to survive, but many lives were lost on both sides. That, and being able to own rather than rent land, contributed to an emigration to America from 1717-1776.[110] But exorbitant rent raises as long-term leases expired (rackrenting) and British economic repression may have been bigger factors.[111]

From 1846-1856, politics and the Great Hunger (potato famine) brought another, mostly Catholic, Irish emigration to America, and turned Irish animosity toward England into a deep, lasting hatred.[112] Most of these immigrants initially went from horrific poverty and religious persecution in Ireland to the same conditions in the slums of America, but emigrating stopped their widespread death by starvation.[113]

Writing a term paper on Ireland's role in World War II led me to conclude that her primary foe was still England. I found a McCabe who was in the Irish Republican Army (IRA). The bomb he reportedly threw into a London subway killed about 50 innocent people.[114] But some Irishmen fought on the allied side and Ireland remained neutral in the war. Also, the Irish exported food to England, allowed flyovers by allied aircraft, and permitted hot pursuit of German submarines in Irish waters. Further, allied personnel interred in "neutral" Ireland often were "allowed" to escape, and most of them were released to the British by 1943.[115]

The Gaelic Irish are more popular in song and legend than the Scotch. But Winston Churchill, England's great World War II leader, had this to say about the Scots:

> *Of all the small nations of this earth, perhaps only the Greeks surpass the Scots in their contribution to mankind.*

A perspective more specific to the American Scotch-Irish[116] follows:

> *With the outbreak of the Revolution in 1775 the Scots-Irish, in interesting contrast to many of their Scottish cousins, were among the most determined adherents of the rebel cause. Their frontier skills were particularly useful in destroying Burgoyne's army in the Saratoga campaign; and George Washington was even moved to say that if the cause was lost everywhere else he would take a last stand among the Scots-Irish of his native Virginia. Serving in the British Army, Captain Johann Henricks, one of the much despised 'Hessians', wrote in frustration 'Call it not an American rebellion, it is nothing more than an Irish-Scotch Presbyterian Rebellion.' It was their toughness, virility and sense of divine mission that was to help give shape to a new nation, supplying it with such diverse heroes as Davy Crockett and Andrew Jackson. They were indeed God's frontiersmen, the real historical embodiment of the lost tribe of Israel.*

Note: not all of the Scotch-Irish were Presbyterians, and some that were may have become Methodists, or Episcopalians, or Baptists, etc.

In his book, *Vernon McCabe* identified descendants of *Sussex County John S. McCabe (1727-1800)*.[117] He also properly eliminated the Owen McCabe who married Catherine Sears (~1745) and his brother James McCabe, who wed Ann Pettigrew (~1750), as close relatives of *1727 John McCabe's* descendants. *Vernon* also noted that DNA analysis might show whether Owen and James had a brother named John who settled in Sussex County. DNA information identified in the McCabe Family DNA Project has since shown that *1727 John McCabe* and those two McCabe brothers do not have a close common ancestor.

Marriage between Ulster-Scots and the Gaelic Irish wasn't unusual[118] and virtually all rural Delmarvans have Irish roots (see Appendix 1). Those include Cannons from Tirconnell (County Donegal) in Ireland's north (west of Ulster), Lynches from western Ireland (County Galway), Quillens from north Ireland (County Antrim), and Timmons from southeastern Ireland (Counties Wicklow and Carlow).

In addition to the Ulster-Scots, gallowglass descendants from outside Ulster emigrated from Ireland to America and can properly be called Scotch-Irish. Descendants of many Scots who emigrated directly to America also fit into that category.

1727 John McCabe has ancestors who were Irish, and Irish Scoti, before becoming Scotch and then returning to Ireland. So it is accurate to call *1727 John* and all his descendants Irish-Scotch-Irish Americans descended from the pagan Irish, then from the Christian Irish, then from the Scotch, and then from gallowglasses in Ireland. As is the case for virtually all people descended from western Europeans, that's a very Celtic ancestry. The Celts from whom we sprang were superior iron workers, farmers, and warriors,[119] and are addressed further in this work under the subject of genetic roots.

McCabe/Mecabe Ancestry

DNA testing shows that I, my fifth cousin *Vernon McCabe*, and *John David Mecabe* (of New Jersey ancestry), have very similar Y Chromosome DNA. The McCabe family DNA Project Coordinator stated (consistent with McCabe Family website information) that the three of us: very probably have a common ancestor within the past 200-300 years; have DNA that is significantly different from the other McCabes tested; and are descendants of Ireland's High King Niall of the Nine Hostages.

As *Vernon McCabe* has historically shown, *John McCabe (1727-1800)* of Sussex County, Delaware is his and my common ancestor. *Brunhilde (Bruni) Wais Mecabe* has traced the *Mecabes* to *Elisha Mecabe* (b. 1799) in Monmouth County, New Jersey. *Elisha's* surname is *McCabe* in most records, including his death certificate.

Information once posted on the internet[120] led to identification (by *Bruni*) of three possible *John McCabe (b. 13 May 1727)* ancestors:[121] James McCabe, b. ~1650, Hugh McCabe, b. ~ 1656, and Thomas McCabe, birth date unknown. No evidence that this Hugh or this James is an ancestor of *1727 John McCabe* has been identified. But Bruni did find the below information (original source not located) on two McCabe brothers, James and John.[122]

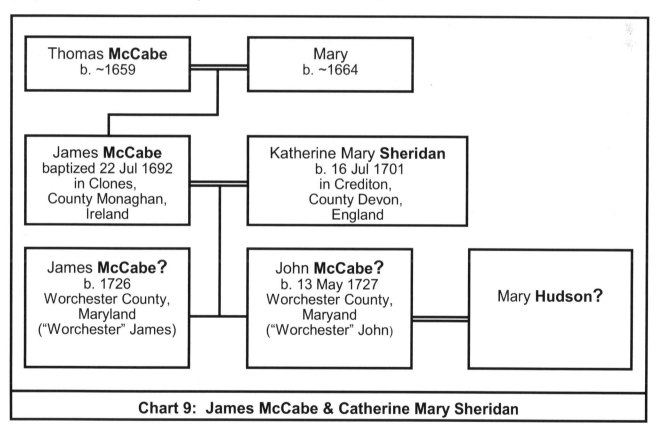

Chart 9: James McCabe & Catherine Mary Sheridan

The information charted incorrectly spells "Worcester" as "Worchester." (That's a likely carryover: there is still a Worchestershire in England.[123]) The present Worcester County, Maryland was formed out of Somerset County on December 17, 1742,[124] over 15 years after *1727 John McCabe* was born, and is directly south of Delaware. A previous Worcester County, Maryland, formed in June 1672, reflected a Maryland claim to land in Delaware, and was located in what is now Sussex County, Delaware.[125] It is the earlier "Worchester" County that information about *1727 John McCabe* appears to refer to.

A "Worchester" County, Maryland John McCabe (b. 13 May 1727) could be Sussex County, Delaware's *John McCabe (13 May 1727- Jan 1800)*. If Sussex County, Delaware's *John McCabe (1727-1800)* did have a brother, that brother could have founded the *Mecabe* family, and the brothers' father could have been the most recent common ancestor of the McCabe-Mecabe branch of the family. But, while there is hard DNA evidence that Sussex County *John McCabe (1727-1800)* had at least one close patrilineal male kin in the progenitor of the Mecabes, he could have been a distant cousin. (Vernon McCabe and I are close patrilineal relatives having very similar male DNA, and we are 5th cousins.)

After defeating O'Neill and the Ulster chieftains in 1603, England did not "plant" County Monaghan. There was some such plantation with English and Scottish families after the Irish Catholic Rebellion and the defeat of the McMahons in 1641, but McCabe is not listed among the more common names of those settlers.

The first census to identify religious affiliation in County Monaghan was in 1861. Roman Catholics were 73% of the population then, Church of Ireland members comprised 14%, and Presbyterians made up 12%. In 1863, McCabe was the sixth most common name in County Monaghan; these were reportedly descendants of gallowglasses imported by the McMahons.[126]

The Church of Ireland was that country's official religion from 1538-1906. (Its U.S. counterpart is the Episcopal Church; both are part of the Anglican Communion.) Church of Ireland birth records for Clones Parish begin in 1682, with Roman Catholic and Presbyterian birth records for Clones starting in 1848 and 1856, respectively.[127]

James and Katherine Mary Sheridan McCabe were reportedly married in Ireland's Kilmore and Ardagh Diocese, Ireland on 16 July 1726.[128] (Kilmore and Ardagh is a Church of Ireland Diocese covering most of northwest Ireland.[129]) Such a marriage could have occurred to facilitate enabling an informally married couple to emigrate. That a son named James was born in "Worchester" County, Maryland the same year seems contraindicated by the hazard of an arduous sea journey to a pregnant woman, but staying in Ireland could have been a bigger worry.

The genetic link between the *Mecabes* and *McCabes* is scientifically solid. But the hypothesis that the sons of the above named James McCabe and Katherine Mary Sheridan are a James McCabe and his brother *1727 John McCabe* (who married *Mary Hudson*) is unconfirmed speculation. That said, County Monaghan or County Cavan are both a likely source of *1727 John McCabe's* and *1799 Elisha Mecabe's* common ancestors. Nearby counties (e.g., Leitrim, Louth, Meath) are also possible sources.

My bet is that, if and when genetic labeling is pursued to the point of identifying the common male ancestry of a large number of present day Ireland's McCabes, and those individuals' ancestry becomes available in the way Vernon McCabe has made ours available, we'll find that our gallowglass ancestors in Ireland lived near but not in Ulster. That's one reason for using the American Scotch-Irish appellation for our genetic ancestry rather than the generic Ulster-Scot name applied in Ireland and England.

John S. McCabe (1727-1800)

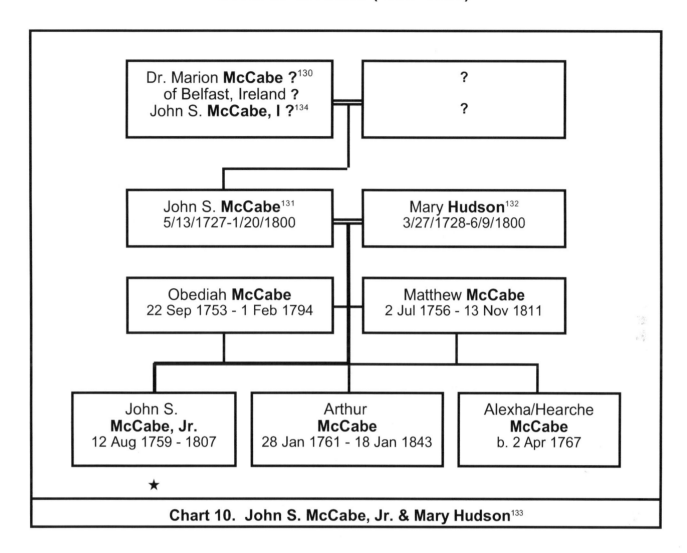

Chart 10. John S. McCabe, Jr. & Mary Hudson[133]

John S. McCabe, Jr.[134] (*1727 John*) married *Mary Hudson* on March 15, 1752. Their sons were 15, 17, 20, and 23 years old, and *John* was 49 when he enlisted (or re-enlisted) in the Continental Army's Delaware Regiment of Foot Soldiers in December 1776. (The Continental Army didn't reject soldiers because of age, and had older ones than him.) *Private John McCabe* served throughout the war and the British surrender at Yorktown on October 19, 1781. And he stayed on at least two months after the peace treaty was signed on September 3, 1783.

At a December 29, 1779 inspection, *Private John McCabe* had a musket, cartridge box, flint, hat, coat, waistcoat, two shirts, breeches, socks, and shoes. And, at a February 1780 inspection, he had a musket, bayonet, cartridge box, 28 cartridges, flint, and bayonet belt. (Not consistently noting coats, blankets, mess kits, canteens, underwear, etc., may have been due to the inspections' nature—or to downplaying the hardships of the Army.)

At the 28-day siege of the Ninety-Six Outpost in South Carolina in 1781, *Private John McCabe* was wounded in the ankle.[135] Unscathed otherwise (as far as we know), he completed his seven years of military service at age 56.

Information passed down via descendants of *Arthur McCabe,* who left Delmarva,[136] states that *1727 John McCabe* was born in "Worchester" County, Maryland.[137] His father is said but not known to have come from Ireland in the early 1700s with three brothers–each reportedly settling in a different place in the colonies.

1727 John settled in the Selbyville, Delaware, area. On 12 April 1748, he purchased a plot of land named Mumford's Choice from William Mumford.[138] (I found no record of an earlier McCabe land transaction and no McCabes on lists of earlier European settlers of the area.)

The *Arthur McCabe* family information also states that *Private John McCabe* was with General Washington when he crossed the Delaware River on December 26, 1776 (along with another Delaware private, three officers, and a doctor), that *1727 John* was in the battle at Germantown, and that he wintered with Washington at Valley Forge.

1727 John's dedication to the revolutionary cause until the very end is consistent with his having joined the fray as early as possible, which would mean that his December 1776 enlistment was actually a re-enlistment. (Documentation of the first enlistment may have been lost or discarded.) It's also possible that *1727 John's* service experience, which was commendable in any case, has been embellished in the retelling.

The *Arthur McCabe* family information also states that the initial pay of a Revolutionary War private was $6.60/month, with no subsistence allowance. In January 1780 it was raised to $13.30 a month, with a $20.00/month subsistence allowance. That represents an oddity of sorts: the privates, who certainly weren't paid enough, were nonetheless paid more than General George Washington, who declined monetary compensation for his service.

None of *1727 John's* four sons fought in the Revolutionary War, and all of them were of an age to do so. There was considerable Tory loyalty to the English crown in Delaware. So one can speculate that a Tory perspective may have kept *1727 John's* sons out of the war. But that's pure conjecture, and *1727 John* may have preferred that he be the soldier and his children not be put at risk. (That's not unusual. I didn't want my son to follow me into military service unless he strongly felt that he should do so, and I feel the same way about my grandsons.)

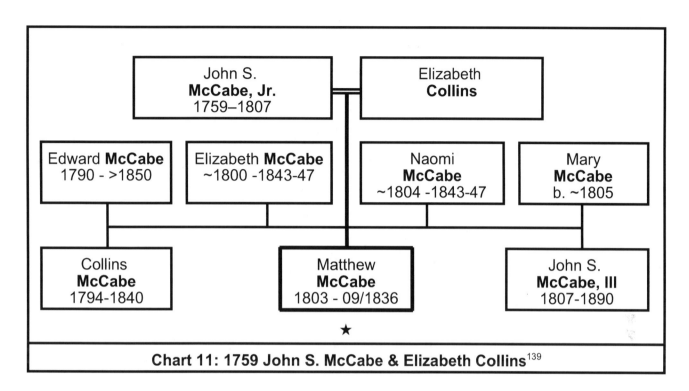

Chart 11: 1759 John S. McCabe & Elizabeth Collins[139]

We know that these 18th and19[th] Century ancestors lacked running water, electricity, and cars–and the time those save. Still, as shown in the below part of the prelude to *The Vision of Sir Launfal*, an 1841 work by American poet James Russell Lowell (1819-1891), their views and their outlook were much like our own.

> *Earth gets its price for what Earth gives us;*
> *The beggar is taxed for a corner to die in,*
> *The priest hath his fee who comes and shrives us,*
> *We bargain for the graves we lie in;*
> *At the Devil's booth are all things sold*
> *Each ounce of dross costs its ounce of gold;*
> *For a cap and bells our lives we pay,*
> *Bubbles we earn with a whole soul's tasking:*
> *'T is heaven alone that is given away,*
> *'T is only God may be had for the asking;*
> *There is no price set on the lavish summer,*
> *And June may be had by the poorest comer.*
>
> *And what is so rare as a day in June?*
> *Then, if ever, come perfect days;*
> *Then Heaven tries the earth if it be in tune,*
> *And over it softly her warm ear lays:*
> *Whether we look, or whether we listen,*
> *We hear life murmur, or see it glisten; ...*

Matthew McCabe (1803-1836)

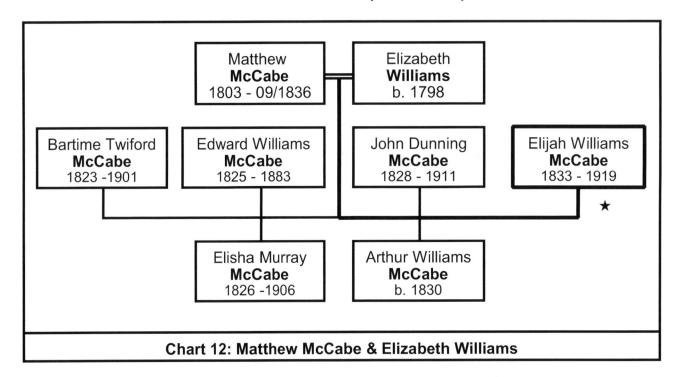

Chart 12: Matthew McCabe & Elizabeth Williams

Elizabeth was five years older than her husband *Matthew*. They had six sons before he died at the age of 33. Three of their children lived into their seventies and eighties. *Edward* died at about age 58. We don't know when *Arthur* died.[140]

Matthew McCabe and his family lived in 19th Century America. That century began with an ongoing controversy over the discrimination between state and federal powers. In 1803, in deciding Marbury v. Madison, the U.S. Supreme Court ruled 6-0 that the Constitution was "the fundamental and paramount law of the nation," and that "an act of the legislature repugnant to the constitution is void."[141] But that didn't resolve the issue. States' rights became a core element of the Civil War (our country's deadliest) and the controversy still persists.

Little has been written about the participation of *1727 John McCabe's* descendant's in war. But war is very important to understanding their (and our) history. It and the freedom it has earned intimately affect us all, including diehard pacifists.

In the early 19th Century, England did not accept that the Revolutionary War gave the USA rights to areas outside the boundaries of its existing states. The British wished to re-establish control over their former colonies. They even stopped our merchant ships on the high seas, asserted that any English-speaking sailors were British subjects, and impressed those men into the British Navy.[142] Also, the United States had let its military strength wane and was too weak to support its desire to conquer Canada.[143] Nonetheless, the impressment of our sailors became the focal point for declaring war against England in 1812.[144] We then tried to invade Canada, but were easily turned back–the British had more, and much more war-hardened, soldiers. But Commodore Oliver Hazard Perry destroyed the British fleet on Lake Erie and the English retreated eastward from Detroit. Other British forces easily took Washington, D.C. and burned most of its government buildings–including the White House. They next marched on Baltimore, but Fort McHenry held (inspiring the writing of the National Anthem) and they drew back. Then Captain Thomas MacDonough destroyed the British Fleet on Lake Champlain, forcing the

10,000 British veterans trying to take New York to return to Canada. There was still a more than 50 ship British Armada, and an army of about 10,000 British regular soldiers, to deal with. They hoped to take New Orleans,[145] control the Mississippi River, and thereby bound our country's westward expansion. But first they had to defeat a self-educated, Scotch-Irish, former Tennessee Militia Major General named Andrew Jackson. His ragtag force of about 4000 was made up of a few U.S. Army regular units; a large group of black, free, former Haitian slaves; Kentucky and Tennessee frontiersmen carrying long rifles, and a band of Jean Lafitte's pirates.

Between the British forces and New Orleans, the quintessentially indomitable Jackson built a six-tenths of a mile long, mud rampart between the Mississippi River and an impassable cypress swamp. His surprise night attack on the British caused them to delay their assault until all their troops were ashore. By then the rampart was very well fortified, and the first British attack was repulsed with the help of broadsides fired from the Mississippi River by the American ship Louisiana. Four days later, the British marched in force against the rampart. They were easy targets and, in about 30 minutes, the senior British General was killed, both his subordinate generals were shot, and there were 2000 British casualties. The U.S. suffered eight dead and 13 wounded. That ended the war. Jackson, idolized for his successes and as a man of the people (See Appendix 3), became a two-term U.S. president, a democratic party founder, and a strong advocate of the primacy of federal over state government.

The War of 1812 has been called the Second War of Independence. It has also been called the Forgotten War, perhaps because the Revolutionary War and the Civil War overshadowed it. But we dare not forget any war. As Appendix 4 shows, war has been and is a continually recurrent aspect of the growth and preservation of the United States.[146] American war deaths now number over one million, three hundred fifteen thousand, seven hundred thirty, and counting (1,315,730+). As the losing side usually does, our enemies have suffered much more than has the United States, but war isn't stopped by horrendous death tolls or enslavement. It remains with us because the nations and people of the world have been and are unable to eliminate it. Moreover, war has been and remains the ultimate means of making and keeping the United States of America sovereign and free. We and our ancestors, including those who did and do not recognize man's inability to avoid war, all have had to come to terms with that. So must our descendants.

Elijah Williams McCabe (1833-1919)

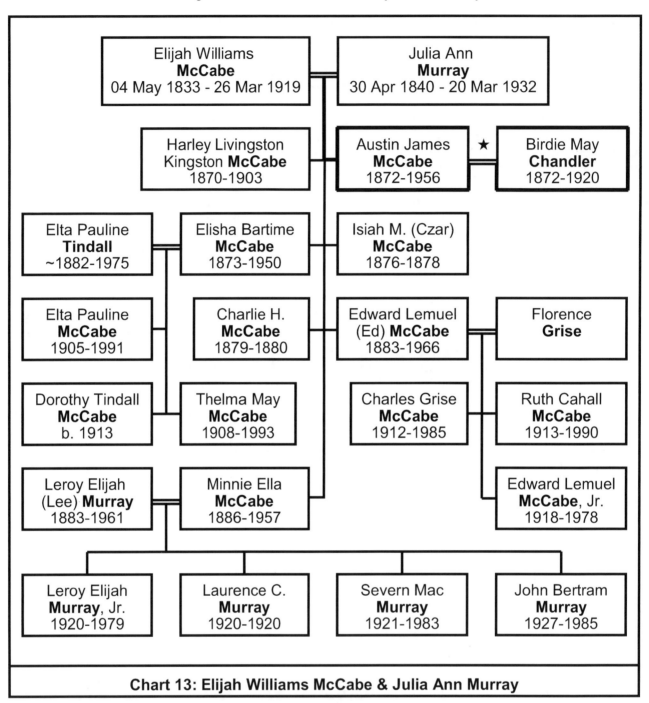

Chart 13: Elijah Williams McCabe & Julia Ann Murray

My Grandfather, *Austin McCabe,* came from Selbyville, Sussex County, Delaware. Several of his family lived on farms beside the road from Selbyville to Fenwick Island, Delaware. Dad spoke of his *Uncle 'Lisha,* but I don't recall him. I do remember being at *Uncle Ed's* farm and playing with the crop of kittens. (Farm cats were valued for rodent control, but tended to become too plentiful.) *Uncle Ed* offered us a kitten we liked, and our parents said OK. So *Uncle Ed* eagerly got a box for us to carry it in–that meant one step back from having to put down the overabundance. But the kitten balked, severely scratched *Uncle Ed's* hand, and fled. We came away empty handed.

Another memory of visiting the Selbyville McCabes is being shown the boar. Their practice was to keep a promising male piglet whole for breeding until his tusks and temperament made him too dangerous. We were warned to stay well clear of this boar because he was approaching that point. I still remember thinking that the danger the boar presented had been understated.

Dad's ebullient *Aunt Minnie*, who took pains to make us welcome, left a lasting memory too. She offered us each an apple from a basketful of that year's pickings, making it a point to choose ones that had rotten spots and cutting those out (to make the supply last longer). Being used to discarding partially rotted food, I didn't want that apple. But my father assured me it was OK and I ate it.

Aunt Minnie held our attention most when we helped her catch a chicken for supper. (At home, that job fell to me and/or my brother because our father wouldn't kill a chicken.) She adeptly wrung the bird's neck with a quick flick of her wrist. Our own hatchet and chopping block method suffered from the unwillingness of the birds to hold still. So the next time Mom decided to cook a chicken at home, we tried *Aunt Minnie's* method. But the birds we experimented on simply un-corkscrewed their heads several turns and ran off. So back to the hatchet and chopping block we went. I never did learn how to wring a chicken's neck.

Two of *Aunt Minnie's* four boys were twins. One, *Laurence*, died when he was 19 days old. The other, *Leroy*, grew up and married *Mary Louise Holton*, the older sister of my high school classmate and friend, *Frank Holton*. *Leroy* and *Mary Louise* settled in Frankford, Delaware. *Frank* and I stopped in from playing to see *Mary Louise* just once. She fed us lunch, thrusting sandwiches at us, and then chided me about my dirty hands when she saw them. I thought she should have given us the chance to wash before proffering the food, but didn't want to risk losing lunch by saying so–*Mary Louise* didn't seem very understanding. *Leroy* I rarely saw, and then only in passing, so I didn't learn anything of note about him.

Austin James McCabe, Sr. (1872-1956)

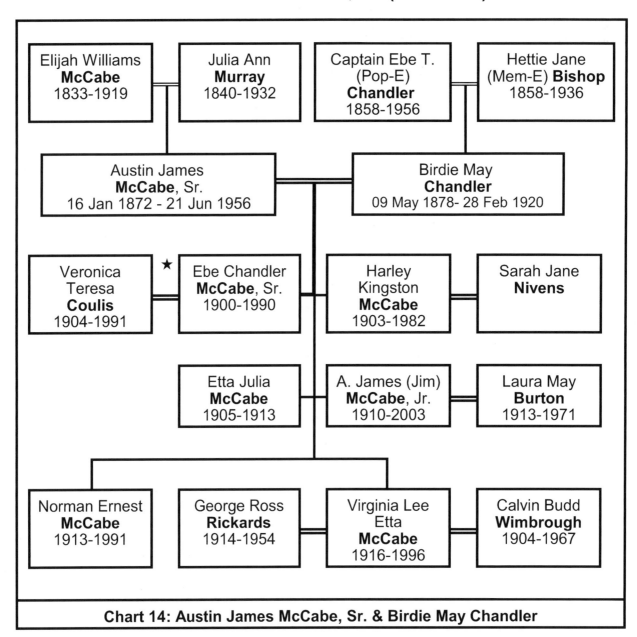

Chart 14: Austin James McCabe, Sr. & Birdie May Chandler

Austin James McCabe, Sr. graduated from Washington College, began medical school, ran out of funds, and left to earn the money to finish. But marriage and a family ended that dream.

Birdie Chandler and her father doted on each other, often walking arm-in-arm. *Pop-E* didn't welcome *Austin* as a suitor, but it's likely that no man could have met his expectations. So *Birdie* and *Austin* eloped. *Pop-E* then moved to Philadelphia to be closer to his work.

Other than her affection for her father and obedience to her mother, information about *Birdie Chandler* hasn't been passed down. But her very close relationship with her father indicates that they had many traits in common. Determination to achieve may have been such a trait.

Austin James McCabe, Sr. became a storekeeper, postmaster, schoolteacher, farm owner, and town alderman. *Etta*, the first daughter, was strikingly lovely[147] and very spoiled. She died from diptheria before her eighth birthday (and my father's 13th). *Dad* told us about the house being quarantined by being roped off. Food was brought to the porch, but the family had to stay inside until the deliverer had departed. *Dad* didn't talk about the death itself until his late 80s. Then, speaking as if it had just happened, he described laying awake at night listening to *Etta* strain to breathe, saying that he "knew that it was over" when that sound stopped one night.

Life went on. Another daughter was born. In February 1920, my father's mother fell behind the house her father had bought for her. She lay unconscious for hours and caught pneumonia. Her parents rushed from Philadelphia to be with her. She died 10 days after her fall. The town knew about the death from hearing her father and his grandsons weeping on the porch.

James and *Norman*, the children *Austin* raised alone, suffered most from their mother's death. My father and *Harley*, being older, were less affected. *Aunt Virginia* lived with her grandparents and was insulated from her father's actions. She thought her mother's death had ended his joy in living, and wouldn't tolerate derogatory statements about him. But *Uncle Jim* told me about seeing his father kicking *Norman* and telling his father that, if he did that again, he'd strike him in the face with his fist. My grandfather asked: "You wouldn't do that, would you?" *Uncle Jim* said that he would and the kicking stopped, at least in his presence.

Uncle Jim said that his father believed that anyone who wasn't sick in bed should be working. My father also depicted my grandfather as a stern taskmaster. That *Austin* became a town alderman more than 10 years after his wife's death showed that he had the respect of the community then. But, by the 1940s, he was disliked for his acrimonious and miserly nature.

Uncle Jim told his daughters about his father picking him and his friends up at school in a horse-drawn sleigh, and driving them all home. And, *Uncle Norman* loved his "Pop" deeply, indicating that rough treatment was only part of the story. Also, *Aunt Virginia* wanted a pony like the ones her friends had. *Pop-E* rejected her pleas, so her father bought one (named Betsy Ross), kept it, and told his daughter to be especially careful while riding because her grandfather would kill him if she got hurt. With my brother and I, though, *Grandpop* was less generous. He often mentioned that, if we were good enough, a pony could be our reward. But no pony ever showed up on our farm, and no explanation of what we had to be better at ever surfaced.

One summer day when I was in *Grandpop's* yard, barefoot, I saw a yellow and brown creature sunning itself in a bare spot under a tree next to the sidewalk, about ten feet from the porch. I called out: "*Grandpop*, there's a big worm out here. Shall I step on it?" My grandfather yelled out that I should get away from it and suddenly burst out of the house. He saw that I was clear, slowly and quietly got a spade, walked over to the sleeping creature and cut off its head. *Grandpop* explained that it was a copperhead snake, took two sticks and pried open its mouth to show me the fangs, and told me that a triangular head meant a snake is poisonous. I was surprised that a two-foot long snake had such a big mouth and fangs, and asked why it had lain straight out instead of coiling up like a rattlesnake, and why the headless body was still moving. *Grandpop* said that copperheads were different from rattlesnakes and that a killed snake's body was said to twitch until sundown. He also said that copperheads travel with their mates, and insisted that he and my father and *Uncle Norman* search for the other snake. He overruled opinions that this copperhead must have been alone and kept them all clearing out underbrush for several hours until the mate was found and killed.

Grandpop, as far as I know, was the last person to keep pigs in Frankford. He had a huge sow. We had to be quiet around her, lest she get frightened and eat her young. He also kept a nanny goat because her milk helped his gastritis. When her milk dried up, nanny had to be bred.

Grandpop had bought a billy goat kid that was ready when needed. Nanny became pregnant, and Billy was butchered. I tasted his meat once. It was incredibly tough.

Grandpop also kept cats–outside. But one had a litter in the house and was allowed to stay there. One day, she was a nuisance, and *Grandpop* told me to put her out. She panicked, clawed my upper lip, got away, and ran back to her kittens. I still have the scars, and the memory of *Mom's* fury with my grandfather.

Another memory is my grandfather's corn crib. It was used to store farm tools. My brother and I were allowed to play with them. *Dad* lectured us for not putting them away properly. We protested because we had put them back neatly and in plain sight. But they weren't in their normal places and *Grandpop* couldn't find them. (I now understand that aspect of older minds.)

Grandpop would have none of my father's practice of shaving with double-edged Gillette blue blades–ones inserted, after one use, through a slot in the rear of the medicine cabinet into the house wall to rust away. My grandfather shaved more ritually, using a soap mug, a shaving brush, and a straight razor honed vigorously on a leather strop, before and during the shaving.

My brother remembers taking our little sister, on a sled, to *Grandpop's* house. He tucked some pennies into her mittens. She lost two of them on the way back. *Grandpop* harassed her about that for months. And two cents weren't worth much even then: a soft drink cost a nickel.

About that time, my grandfather asked me to try a math problem that he used to give his students. It went something like: if the head of a fish is half as long as the tail and the body of the fish is three times as long as the head, and the fish is three feet long, how long is each part? Pleased that I figured it out, *Grandpop* said his students hadn't been able to and asked me how much money I had. I counted out my net worth–97¢. *Grandpop* said I deserved a reward, and gave me three pennies so I'd have a dollar.

On the farm, *Grandpop* and *Uncle Norman* came to dinner on Sundays. *Grandpop* would walk around with me and/or my brother to explain about farming. He once asked me if I liked kale, which he pointed out growing along the ditch bank. I said I didn't. He told me that I should because it was free. *Grandpop* told my brother the same thing about poke berries, explaining that the purple berries the birds ate were poisonous to us, but the leaves were OK. Neither I nor my brother have eaten poke leaves. But we never went hungry, and I think *Grandpop* did.

I also recall hearing that it cost money to heat water, so bathing should be done in a few inches of it and not in a tubful. It wasn't my grandfather who said that, but someone else in his generation–showing that *Grandpop's* frugality wasn't atypical.

I often pretended to drive my grandfather's ramshackle, red, 1938 Dodge pickup. The foot-operated button on the left had no apparent purpose. Grandpop and *Uncle Norman* said it didn't do anything. But I kept asking and they found out that it was the headlight dimmer switch. (Driver's licenses were easier to get then.)

Grandpop's parlor had a wind-up Victrola and some old records. We played *"A Tisket, A Tasket"* and "*Playmate*" on it interminably. There was a piano there too. I remember it as being polished and dust-free, which was unique in the house. My sister *Phyllis*, at about the age of five, began listening to tunes on the radio and playing them well on the piano. So *Mom* found the money for music lessons. The teacher required endlessly practicing the scales and cured my sister of piano playing in two weeks. *Phyllis* now has no memory of ever having played the piano.

There was also an organ in *Grandpop's house*, unpolished but working. It wasn't like *Grandpop* to keep anything he didn't value. I asked my father about the piano and organ. He said they had been my grandmother's, and that she was musically talented and had been sought after to play at church and other events around the county.

On summer evenings, my grandfather's porch was cool and refreshing. The grownups sat there–talking and being comfortable. My brother and I collected enough lightning bugs to make a jar glow dimly. We only kept them for a short time. They don't glow for long in jars and the ambiance they added was nicer when they were twinkling about the yard with the stars and moon and street lamps the only other lights around. (The kerosene lamps in the house were out and could be lit only by and in rooms occupied by adults. Being sent inside to get something in the dim light that came through the windows could be a painfully sticky experience because flypaper coils abounded in the house.) I also remember how clear and still the evening was there. It was rare for a car to come by, but if one did, its engine noise reached our ears long before we could see it. When it had gone, chirping insects were the only background sound.

My father believed that his mother died because his father made her return to work in the store and post office too soon after she had the flu in 1918. When his father was abed dying of prostate cancer, *Dad* berated him for killing "*Mom*" until *Aunt Virginia* said "*Ebe*, that's enough!" For the rest of his life, *Dad* had nightmares about that. But I think all of *Austin's* sons, except *Norman*, shared my father's view, and that my grandfather was deeply affected by their feelings and his own guilt. *Grandmom's* determination may have caused her to be up and about when she shouldn't have been. But *Grandpop* had to have known that *Grandmom* had been ill for over a year, and should have made sure she rested until she regained her health.

Grandpop occasionally visited and talked quietly and companionably with *Pop-E*. Their caring about *Birdie*, and aloneness, probably brought them together.

I still wonder why my grandfather behaved the way he did. His and *Aunt Minnie's* frugality indicate they were taught that. Disappointment about medical school may have had a lasting effect. *Etta's* untimely death was a harsh blow. *Uncle Norman* needed care that Grandpop couldn't provide, and that was a lasting strain. *Aunt Virginia* may have been right about *Birdie's* loss taking the heart out of him. His benevolent father-in-law had the adoration of *Austin's* sons, especially my father, and *Grandpop's* agenda caused him to be seen quite differently by them. But the copperhead snake incident showed that he was capable of being a much better man: he effectively resolved the problem and explained the danger in an instructive and positive way. Also, there was caring evident in his keeping Betsy Ross for *Aunt Virginia*. Had his lot and luck and upbringing been different, *Grandpop* might have been much nicer.

After *Birdie* died and his children, except for *Norman*, grew up and left, *Grandpop* was pretty much alone until my father moved back to Frankford. He didn't show it, but it brightened *Grandpop's* life to have a son and grandchildren nearby. When, after about 10 years, *Dad* moved his family to Salisbury, Maryland, *Grandpop* went back to his more lonely life.

My wondering about my grandfather has increased since I saw my face as his visage when I was shaving several years ago. (I still see similarities.) Underneath, *Grandpop* probably suffered at least as much as those he alienated. He apparently never recovered from the blows life dealt him, and built a growing resentment that made him more sour and vindictive over the years. But, all I know for certain is that the most pleasure I ever saw him show was the 3¢ worth my solving his math problem brought. The wealth he put together, and left, was meaningless. His life was unsuccessful. And that's sad.

Harley Kingston McCabe (1903-1982)

Uncle Harley was talented, generous, and exceptionally popular. After graduating from the University of Delaware and Harvard Law School, he failed the Delaware bar exam. My father said that was because the state bar was under Republican control and we were a family of Democrats. My suspicion is that *Uncle Harley* wasn't interested in practicing law and didn't prepare well for the exam. He found a career he liked, advancing to Vice-President and Product Manager of the Chamberlain Rock Wool Company.

When *Uncle Harley* was around, a steady stream of people dropped in to see him or phoned. He reveled in that. I particularly recall him taking a phone call from a lady he had known years earlier. He talked animatedly and delightedly for some time. After the call, he grinned broadly and said: *I **love** it when a woman calls me.*

Uncle Harley once visited just after I had gotten my first driver's license. He put me behind the wheel of his new Cadillac convertible, much to my delight, and his.

Single life suited *Uncle Harley*–he didn't marry until he was 48 years old. His wife, *Jane Nivens*, was very bright and articulate, strikingly lovely, impeccably groomed, trim, shapely, extremely personable, and a successful business owner. Her daughter *Terry* and *Uncle Harley* were very fond of each other. It seemed a good match, but the marriage didn't last. My mother felt that *Uncle Harley* married to settle down, while *Jane* wanted excitement and things many years of very hard work had denied her. But neither of them may have been able to adapt to marriage after being quite successful on their own.

Mom kept *Terry* informed about her stepfather–*Uncle Harley* was an infrequent communicator.

Some years after *Uncle Harley* retired, he moved to an apartment near my parents' home. A few years later, he moved to a nearby nursing home because of Parkinson's Disease. There, his body deteriorated and his speech became increasingly slurred. He turned his finances over to my father. Eventually, only close family visited, and only *Dad* could understand him. When *Uncle Harley* began falling out of chairs and out of bed, he was tied to a chair during the day and to his bed at night. That upset him deeply.

During my father's last visit, *Uncle Harley's* speech was so slurred that even *Dad* couldn't understand it. After unsuccessfully striving to communicate, *Uncle Harley* lay back in bed, closed his eyes, and became unresponsive. *Dad* left soon afterwards. The home called a few hours later to say that *Uncle Harley* was gone. My father felt that his brother "just gave up and died."

Unfortunately, *Uncle Harley's* deterioration and demise were a painfully clear case of dying being better than living. That agonizing end notwithstanding, most of his 78 years were happy ones, and he brightened a lot of lives along the way.

A. James McCabe, Jr. (1910-2003)

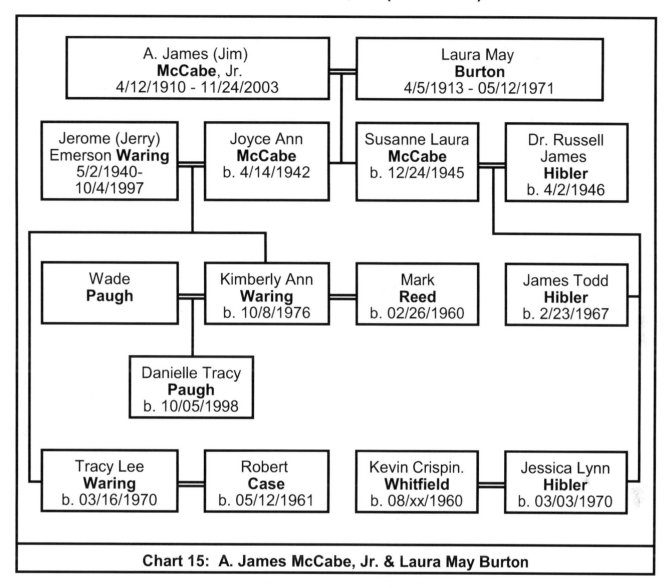

Chart 15: A. James McCabe, Jr. & Laura May Burton

Uncle Jim was nine years old when his mother died. By the time he was 13, he was buying all the produce sold in his father's store. At 16, he was loading railroad cars with strawberries. He went to sea at the age of 19 on the S.S. Katrina Lurckenback, a coastal steamer, working in the engine room and visiting east and west coast ports. Then he worked for transportation inspection services at loss/damage work, claims, supervising loading, and inspecting food, trees, furniture, paper, coal, and transport equipment. In 1936 he started the McCabe Inspection Service in New York City. When he was 46, his company was inspecting 32,000 truck and railroad car loads of fresh fruits and vegetables a year. *Uncle Jim* also bought farms. He said land was the best investment because the population grew but the amount of land didn't.

Uncle Jim was what my father called a graduate of the school of hard knocks. He worked at the docks and freight yards. The tales he related included a robbery attempt by thugs who tried to run him off the road near his work. He rammed their car off the street with his, and drove on. And, he had a .357 Magnum revolver just in case. The financial hurdles were tough too. *Uncle Jim* told me that he had been "bankrupt" several times but was the only one who knew and he came out OK. (*Susanne*, his younger daughter, told me later that his family did know, they just didn't discuss it with him.)

When I was preparing to go to college, *Uncle Jim* asked me about the tuition and how I was paying for it. I told him it was $400 and I had saved up the money. He told me where I could buy two ocean-front lots in Ocean City, Maryland with that, continue working, and invest in beach property that would pay off more than a college education. A high rise ocean-front hotel (the Carousel) went up right there about 20 years later, and a few years after that single lots nearby were selling for over a million dollars each, verifying his assessment of the financial opportunity.

Astute investing and hard work made *Uncle Jim* wealthy, and good fortune shone on him when he married *Laura May Burton,* a registered nurse. *Aunt Laura* was wonderful. She died in her 50s, and *Uncle Jim* never stopped mourning her. Once, when I visited him at the farm he retired to in Dover, Delaware, he played the role of an active widower, and talked about all the ladies interested in him. But, when I said that he wasn't going to find another "*Aunt Laura,*" he quietly and sadly responded "I know." We didn't speak about that again.

My first memories of *Uncle Jim* are from New York City. He was tolerant of boyish behavior. An example was a visit to see his new apartment. My brother and I rode the building's elevators until the superintendent complained. Dad scolded us, but *Uncle Jim* said that the superintendent shouldn't have said anything.

Uncle Jim kept in touch with relatives and commissioned a family genealogy (identifying the McCabe name source as "Son of the Helmeted One"). Unfortunately, the records of that are gone.

In his 80s, *Uncle Jim* was banged up in a fall from a sled. He told me that one of his daughters, upset that he was sledding, had asked him when he was going to grow up, and that he answered: *Never, I hope.*

Uncle Jim once asked me if I'd like to have the no longer used over-and-under shotguns he had bought for himself and *Aunt Laura*. (They were very nice guns.) I said that I didn't hunt any more and it would better if they went to someone who would use them. *Uncle Jim* was disappointed (he enjoyed giving people things).

At the age of 93, *Uncle Jim* became ill and died in a few days. He lived longer than his siblings, was successful, and his home and heart were always open.

Norman Ernest McCabe (1913-1991)

My *Uncle Norman* was amiable, generous and well liked. There was nothing mean about him, but he had a learning disability. His father's mistreatment may have been a factor. The loss of his mother may have contributed. But it wasn't inability to assimilate facts. He had a multitude of those at hand.

The hand-me-down story about *Uncle Norman's* birth is that it happened very quickly, without warning. His father held the child and sent for the doctor. *Uncle Norman* was reportedly deprived of air long enough to affect brain function.

Uncle Norman didn't graduate from high school and didn't find work until later in life. He was then employed by the State Highway Department, doing menial tasks and taking pride in supporting himself. Later, he entered an adult education program and received his high school diploma at about the age of 62.

My mother once commented that, as long as *Norman* had money, no child in town had to go without ice cream. I promptly tested that. *Mom* had overstated the case. (I think I would have gotten the ice cream if my sister *Phyllis* had been along. *Uncle Norman* was particularly fond of her, and she returned his affection in kind.)

Aunt Virginia called *Norman* "Nornie," which is no doubt the way she first learned to speak his name. And *Nornie* never paid attention to housekeeping. So *Aunt Virginia*, and/or my mother, and/or my sister *Phyllis* periodically went over and cleaned up when things got too bad for their sensibilities.

Relatives, and especially *Uncle Jim*, often gave *Uncle Norman* gifts of clothing. He accepted them politely, but felt no obligation to wear them. I once went into an unused upstairs bedroom in his house and found stacks of gift shirts, still boxed and still inside the unopened, clear wrappings they had come in.

Norman McCabe lived in the house he grew up in, on the corner of Main and Thatcher Streets in Frankford, Delaware, until it burned down, and then lived next door on Thatcher Street. The community was fond of him. When he was mugged and beaten, in his later years, by a member of the community's minority group, the whole town, including the rest of the minority group, was outraged.

My *Uncle Norman* loved his family, was kind to others, and was trustworthy with children. He never married. He amassed no wealth. His life was inherently lonely, but he stayed positive and enthusiastic. Overall, I think of him as being more successful than his father was.

Virginia Lee Etta McCabe (1916-1996)

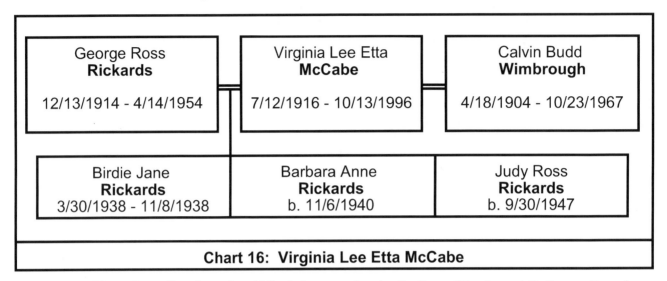

George Ross **Rickards** 12/13/1914 - 4/14/1954	Virginia Lee Etta **McCabe** 7/12/1916 - 10/13/1996	Calvin Budd **Wimbrough** 4/18/1904 - 10/23/1967
Birdie Jane **Rickards** 3/30/1938 - 11/8/1938	Barbara Anne **Rickards** b. 11/6/1940	Judy Ross **Rickards** b. 9/30/1947

Chart 16: Virginia Lee Etta McCabe

Like many Chandler offspring, *Aunt Virginia* was physically tiny. She loved Bethany Beach as a child, but "turned blue" from staying in the water too long. Her remedy for that was to lie down and cover herself in sun-baked sand until the shaking stopped and she could avoid being rebuked by *Mem-E*.

Aunt Virginia lost her mother when she was three years old, and was raised by strict but indulgent grandparents, in a very nice home. Her father lived just down the street with her brothers *James* and *Norman,* whose lives were much less pleasant. That prepared *Uncle Jim* for having to fend for himself, but he resented his sister's easier life, and made that very clear to her. Still, being pampered as a child had no obvious ill effect on *Aunt Virginia's* character, though she did use her children (and my father's) as step-and-fetch-it assets.

When my mother went to the hospital to give birth to my brother, *Aunt Virginia* was enlisted to tend to me, a 22-month-old. She was 18 years old and had no experience with children. My father was no help–he was busy celebrating the birth of his second son. Aunt Virginia, known to her brothers as "Sister," was totally frustrated in her new role. She and I were alone when I forlornly looked at her and said: *Mommy don, Daddy don, aw tister*. She hugged me and we both cried. That began our lasting affection for each other.

Aunt Virginia, at the age of 18, married *George Ross Rickards*. Two and a half years later, their daughter *Jane* was born. I only vaguely recall little *Jane* but remember my parents' grief when she died (at the age of eight months). My cousin *Barbara* was born two years later. She and my sister often stayed overnight with each other. My brother and I didn't look forward to *Barbara's* visits. The girls giggled much of the night, disrupting our sleep, and *Barbara* was snippy about our complaints. To this day, I am perplexed about how giggling girls grow up and become good people.

My cousin *Judy* arrived almost seven years after *Barbara*. Because she was younger, I had relatively little contact with her.

Barbara's and Judy's families are shown in the following.

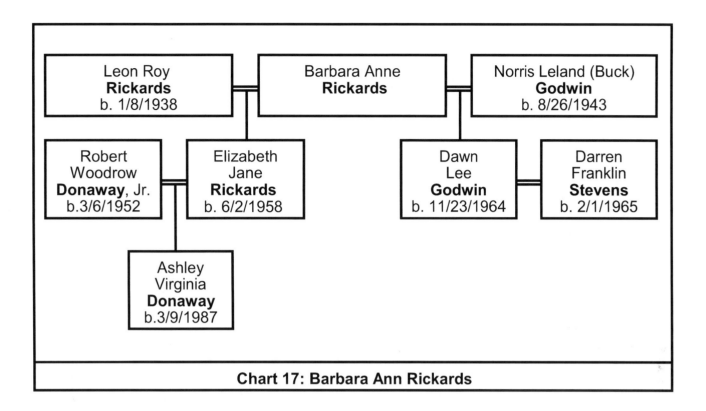

Chart 17: Barbara Ann Rickards

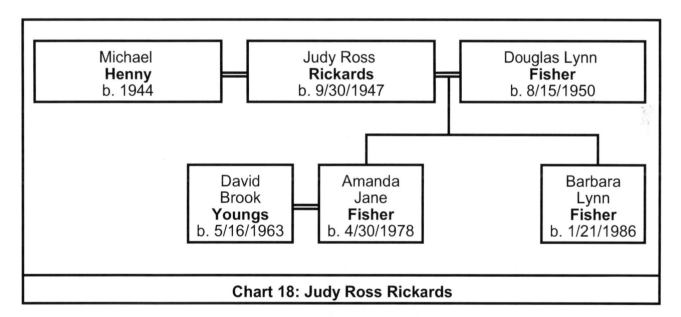

Chart 18: Judy Ross Rickards

Judy was six years old and *Barbara* was 14 when their father died. I remember my mother and father going to visit him in the hospital. *Mom* asked to take a little ceramic figurine I had to him. It was about three inches long and had a loose head with a long tongue that impudently popped out when the figurine was shaken. *Mom* said that *George Ross* laughed when he worked it.

Barbara's and *Judy's* father was active and personable. He impressed us by doing things like drive in harness horse races. But the clearest memory I have of him is of his driving both our families to a movie. On the return trip, we were alone on the highway when a car wheel appeared on the road ahead of us, going the same way we were. There was a bemused discussion of where it had come from until *Uncle George Ross* realized it was from his own car. He stopped without incident, retrieved the wheel, put it back on, and we returned home.

The movie we saw that night, a western, stuck in my mind. I remembered its title and the lead actor. A couple of years ago, I related those to *Barbara*. She emphatically asserted that the actor I named wasn't in that movie, and named the one who starred in it. So I looked it up and found that *Barbara* was right.

After *Uncle George Ross* passed on, *Aunt Virginia* suffered from not having been trained to support herself. She became a waitress at Woody's Diner in Selbyville, Delaware. That wasn't an easy life. But she met *Calvin Wimbrough* there, and they became friends and married. He was a fine person, respected and liked by his in-laws. So *Aunt Virginia* married, and outlived, two fine men. After that, she had a good friend, *Dalmas James Parker*, for many years, but lived alone.

My mother and father played cards with Aunt *Virginia* and *Dalmas,* with but one instance (to my knowledge) of any lack of harmony. That occurred after *Mom* and *Dad* visited *Aunt Virginia* at her home in Berlin, Maryland. *Mom* remarked that *Aunt Virginia* had been too busy tidying up all the time—even emptying out and washing each ash tray as soon as just one cigarette was stubbed out in it. (*Mom* was not a meticulous housekeeper, and my father and his sister were both fastidious in their habits.) *Dad*, unaware that a storm was brewing, prompted the first thunderclap by replying that his sister had always been neat and clean—it was in her blood. It took a few days for *Mom* to regain her equanimity, but no card playing evenings were missed as a result.

My last communication with *Aunt Virginia* was by phone when she was in the hospital. I knew she was seriously ill, and was afflicted with bedsores. I asked when I could visit her. She convincingly said, in a normal voice, that she was doing fine and I shouldn't make a special trip. So I didn't. She died a few days later.

Ebe Chandler McCabe, Sr. (1900-1990)

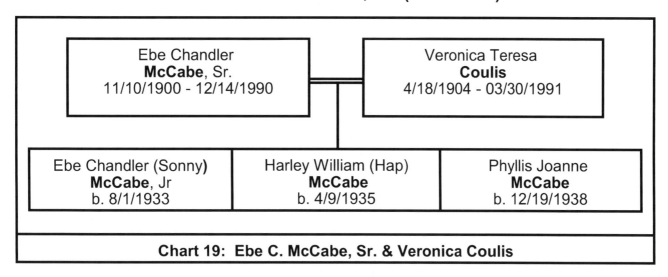

Ebe Chandler **McCabe**, Sr. 11/10/1900 - 12/14/1990		Veronica Teresa **Coulis** 4/18/1904 - 03/30/1991
Ebe Chandler (Sonny) **McCabe**, Jr b. 8/1/1933	Harley William (Hap) **McCabe** b. 4/9/1935	Phyllis Joanne **McCabe** b. 12/19/1938

Chart 19: Ebe C. McCabe, Sr. & Veronica Coulis

My father had much of *Pop-E's* quickness, strength, and dexterity. His passion was baseball. *Uncle Jim* said that he could have "done something" with his baseball skills if he had pursued them. Their father had no use for baseball and tried to keep his sons at work on the farm. His own availability was limited by his duties as postmaster and store keeper, and *Dad* regularly skipped out to play ball.

Dad was the first student in his school to go through 12 years of school (instead of 11), and was the only 12th grade student. He often told children that he graduated both first and last in his high school class, leaving them to figure out how.

After high school, *Dad* went to college, and left without telling anyone. When I went to the University of Delaware, I didn't write home much. *Mom* and *Dad* thought I might have done the same thing that *Dad* did and called the Dean. He summoned me to his office for a chiding. I wrote more often after that.

Dad went back to school (Drexel University) to become a surveyor, and worked on the Reading Railroad crew that laid out the route from Philadelphia to New York City. He was laid off during the Depression and couldn't get other work because employers felt he would go back to the railroad when things opened up. After a stint in bread delivery, *Dad* delivered milk to Bala Cynwyd in a horse-drawn wagon, a job gained by claiming to be just off the farm and lasting until we left Philadelphia.

Dad and *Mom* met through *Mom's* best friend, *"Aunt" Martha*, my Godmother, and often mentioned that they had their first date at the Mastbaum theater in Philadelphia. (They were outraged when it was torn down.)

Aunt Martha and *Mom* came from Buffalo, New York to Philadelphia together, and worked at the Curtis Publishing Company. *Aunt Martha's* spouse was *Beecher Finch*. Dad admired *Beecher* for enlisting in the army in World War I and rising to the rank of Captain, and for his cleverness. After the war, *Beecher,* who may have had a military pension, decided he wasn't going to work for a living. *Dad* said *Beecher* did things like modify his coal furnace grate to heat his home with one-quarter of the coal most people used. *Aunt Martha* and *Beecher* had a son *Richard,* who died young, probably while still in his 30s. The other thing that sticks in my mind about them is their pet turtle. It was kept downstairs, where there were few rugs (turtles cannot be housebroken).

In Philadelphia, we lived in Germantown, near *Hugo* and *Bea Wolfe*. The *Wolfes*, a Jewish family, owned the Uptown Camera and Sports Shop. *Mom* and *Bea* were close friends. *Bea* helped out when my brother was born, and when *Mom* was caring for my brother when he had rheumatic fever. Long after we left Philadelphia, when I was in my teens, a package of toys and games from the *Wolfes* arrived at our house each year as Christmas presents. We once visited the *Wolfes* in Philadelphia, and their sons *Bobby* and *Henry* came to stay about a week with us in Delaware. This family friendship didn't keep us from exposure to anti-Semitism, but it did show us how wrong it is.

When I was a two-year-old, *Mom* repainted the kitchen furniture white with red trim. She then went grocery shopping, leaving *Hap* and me in *Dad's* care. On her return, she saw that I had found the paint brushes and embellished the furniture's red trim. *Hap* was in his crib playing with the turpentine-soaked white paint brush. *Dad* was asleep. The sheets around him were decorated with streaks of red paint. *Mom* decided that my brother was OK, retrieved the brushes, read my father the riot act, and decided to punish me. *Dad* got me off by saying he had already done that. But I was the culprit in *Mom's* recountings. (*Dad* didn't bring it up.)

That same year, my tonsils were removed and my ear abscesses were lanced. In addition, while "riding" the arm of a rocking chair and playing "Lone Ranger," I upended the horse and the point of a rocker tore loose the tips of my left index and middle fingers. *Mom* rushed me to Temple University Hospital and was told the fingers had to be amputated at the first joint. She refused and rushed me to see *Dr. Spots, Pop-E's* doctor. He sewed the tips back on and checked them often. *Mom* described my reaction to seeing him as being to say "Hello, Dr. Pots," and bursting into tears. I still think about how good a doctor he was, and about how I developed a lasting apprehension about doctors and hospitals. (I walked into the Philadelphia Naval Hospital in my 40s and broke out into a cold sweat upon smelling ether, and my blood pressure still goes up in the doctor's office.)

The railroad job didn't re-open. In 1937, we moved to New York City, where *Dad* went to work inspecting fruit for *Uncle Jim*. *Dad* went first. The rest of us followed in the moving van. Being in it is my only conscious memory of having lived in Philadelphia.

In New York, we lived in Astoria, on 44th Street. From the building roof we could see the 1939 World's Fair Trylon and Perisphere. We also went to Laguardia Field to watch the seaplanes ("China Clippers") land out by Flushing Meadows. The Yankee Clipper often flew over and seeing it was considered special.

My parents, like most of America, were very upset about the 1932 kidnaping and murder of the 20-month old son of Charles "Lucky Lindy" Lindbergh, who became a national hero by becoming the first pilot to fly solo across the Atlantic.[148] A German immigrant carpenter, Bruno Hauptman, was executed for the crime in 1936. *Mom* and *Dad* talked about the murder for many years, expressing dismay that fame could foster such tragedy.

My father took delight in a 1938 airplane flight by Douglas "Wrong Way" Corrigan, who flew from Long Beach, California to New York, filed a return flight plan to Long Beach, and then flew to Ireland instead. Corrigan was a skilled aircraft mechanic, one of the builders of Charles Lindbergh's *Spirit of St. Louis*, and had modified his own plane for transatlantic flight. He had been denied permission to fly nonstop from New York to Ireland, and claimed that the transatlantic flight was due to navigational error caused by heavy cloud cover obscuring landmarks and low light conditions resulting in misreading his compass. Wrong Way never admitted to deliberately flying to Ireland.[149]

My sister was born in New York. I remember liking the name "*Phyllis,*" and being happy when she was named that. It was probably when *Mom* was in the hospital for her birth that my brother and I found some Christmas presents in a closet–little "Popeye" flashlights. *Mom* found out and returned them to the store.

My brother and I caught chicken pox in New York. I still remember its intense misery, and having to let the "lady doctor" who came to the apartment examine me.

Mom sent us to bed at 7 p.m. in New York. I lay there, wide-awake, listening to the kids playing outside. But she was totally intractable about the matter.

My mother forbid fighting and I was continually beaten up by the neighborhood kids. *Dad* wasn't aware because it happened when he was asleep (fruit inspection, like milk delivery, was night work). But I came home beaten up one day when *Dad* was up, the no fighting rule changed, and I responded in kind to the treatment I had received. On my side of the street, I was successful with one qualification. *Woocko Shafer,* who ran away from fights, fought and came out ahead if cornered. So I learned to chase but not catch him. I also learned the advantage of being on one's own sidewalk. Another boy, smaller and even skinnier than I was, lived across the street. On my side he was no threat. On his side, he won if we fought. We both avoided crossing the street.

The fighting stopped when the new pecking order was established. An exception was *Woocko's* brother *Collie*. He once, when I was returning from the corner store with my arms full of groceries, ran out of the alley, knocked me and the groceries down, and fled. *Mom* asked why I and the groceries were such a mess. She didn't believe my explanation, fueling my outrage. *Collie* ran slowly, so I was able to retaliate vigorously. One day his mother intervened. Someone must have told *Mom* because she came out of the building while *Collie's* mother was holding me for him to hit. *Mom* put a quick stop to that with a few words. *Collie* and his mother went inside. After that, when I came out, he got off the street.

Our school in New York was Public School 70 (PS-70). I remember the music teacher having each child sing for her. She told me that, when we sang in assembly, I should mouth the words without letting them come out. That also applied during air raid drills, when we sat on the cool marble floor of the hallway, next to the wall, with the lights out, while the teachers led us in song.

A dictatorial PS-70 teacher made penmanship an unpleasant experience. And, the reading teacher said I would never learn to read if I didn't pay attention, prompting me to say that I already could. (*Dad* had unknowingly taught me by reading the newspaper comics aloud while I sat on his lap.) So she handed me a book and told me to read it out loud. I did. She was displeased, and her demeanor from then on continued to increase my dislike for school.

My brother and I walked to school in Astoria. There was a Catholic school on the way, and an Irish kid forbade us from going by "his" school. He was bigger and huskier and had to be reckoned with. But he listened when I said we had to get to our school, and gave us an acceptable way past his–on the other side of the street with no dallying. So that's the route my brother and I took every day.

Mom was very unhappy about her kids being brought up in the city, and *Dad* moved us to Frankford, Delaware when I was in the Fourth Grade. Initially, the arrival of a "city kid" there was disruptive. The movers had just started unloading when *Asher Lee Dukes* challenged me to a fight. I won but was angry because he had pulled my hair–that was unfair. *Mom* blamed and scolded me, and sent me to my grandfather's house (on the next block) to settle down. There I met *Sewell Franklin*, a lanky kid taller than I was, and intent on putting the city kid in his place.

During our fight *Sewell* grabbed a straw broom and hit me with it. The wire binding the straw tore through my T-shirt and drew blood from my shoulder. I grabbed the broom and chased *Sewell* home. He ran inside. I dared him to come out and fight. His mother came to the door and sent me home instead.

The fights continued until *Richard Bunting*, who was a year or two older, won our fight. That established the new pecking order and ended my fighting in Frankford. My father's attitude toward fighting did change though–he repeatedly reminded me that there was only one heavyweight boxing champion of the world, and that he only held the title for a few years.

We were promptly accepted in Frankford. Its people already knew my father, my grandfather, and my great-grandfather. Adjustment to school didn't take long either. The most significant change was corporal punishment, prohibited in New York but not in Delaware. My first teacher there, *Ms. Edna Morris*, had a well-sanded, well-varnished, ~2' long, ~3" wide paddle. On its back was a sanded, varnished lathing strip, attached near the handle by a hinge. It punctuated the paddle's use with a resounding smack. After about a week at school, *Ms. Morris* said that my father had to be paddled when he was a boy and now I needed it. (She and *Dad* were close in age and knew each other when they were children.) So she bent me over her desk and paddled my bottom. That didn't hurt much physically–*Ms. Morris* didn't punish in anger or whack hard. But she got the desired deportment change.

Dad's first job in Frankford was at the Post Office. He often enlisted me to cancel the stamps on outgoing mail, using a cantankerous machine that always seemed to be painfully squashing my fingers. I dreaded every session.

Flimsy, single-sheet V-Mail was used to write to servicemen during the war.[150] The letter was written on one side and the sheet was folded into and mailed as an envelope. V-mail was later microfilmed, sent overseas, reprinted, and delivered. The process made more space available for shipping war materials.

U.S. War Bonds brought in $187.5 billion to support the war. Over 85 million Americans invested in them–an achievement not matched before or since.[151]

One of the first things I noticed in Frankford was the gold stars displayed on similar window hangings in several houses. Dad explained that the gold star designated the wife or mother of a serviceman who had been killed in World War II, and that the family living there was to be treated with special respect and consideration. That view was uniformly shared throughout the town.

During WWII, car headlight top halves were painted black so as to not be visible from the air, and house windows were supposed to be shaded at night (a blackout) so enemy aircraft couldn't use their light to navigate. Also, there were watch towers at the beach for searching for submarines. If they saw any, we didn't learn about it. But we did see, and feel, tar on the beach from oil tanker sinkings. It lasted for years, was painful on the skin, and was hard to get off.

Rationing was another WWII experience, with coupons for flour, sugar, coffee, meats, canned fish, gasoline, etc. *Dad* became the head of the local OPA (Office of Price Administration). There was community gossip about under-the-table payments for chicken crops and about suppliers overcharging, but discussing the black market or coupon trading was forbidden at home. Rationing wasn't a great hardship for rural Delaware–near self-sufficiency in food production saw to that.

Some WWII Prisoners of War were used as workers at Eagle Poultry. We occasionally watched them being dropped off or picked up. There was also a DP (Displaced Person) in Frankford. DPs were WWII victims from Nazi concentration camps, labor camps, POW camps, etc.[152] This one, a Latvian, worked for *Clifton Brasure*, a chicken feed store owner, at the same time my father did. He was a strong, cheerful young man with an intense craving for coca-cola.

Delaware provided school busses only for kids who lived outside town limits. Our school was outside the town, and children who lived closer to it than we did, but outside Frankford's boundary, were bussed to school. We had to walk about two miles to school. That made for a permanent distaste for form over substance bureaucracy. It wasn't until we moved outside the town limits, at about the same distance from school as before, that we rode the school bus back and forth.

When my sister *Phyllis* was about six years old, *Dr. Long* diagnosed her as having infantile paralysis (Polio). *Mr. Murray* had someone drive his school bus route and drove *Mom*, *Dad*, and *Phyllis* to the Sister Kenny Center in Wilmington, Delaware. *Phyllis* was there about a week before the diagnosis was confirmed, and *Hap* and I were quarantined at home for a couple of weeks while she was ill. Our milk delivery then was six quarts every other day, and we had to keep the empty bottles until the quarantine was lifted. Hap and I once went to Wilmington with our parents to visit *Phyllis*, but weren't allowed to see her because we were too young to go in.

Our home in Frankford was heated by a wood stove. At bedtime, the air inlet and stovepipe damper were closed down to make the fire last longer. But the house was still icy cold each winter morning. As the oldest child, it was my duty to restart the fire before *Mom* got up to make breakfast. It didn't take long to master doing that speedily and get back into bed until breakfast was ready.

Farm life was warmer in winter. The hard coal (anthracite) fire lasted overnight. But the stove was in the dining room and its heat didn't circulate well to the upstairs. *Mom* wanted to remove half the wall between the living and dining rooms to fix that. *Dad* said that the ceiling would fall down without the wall. *Mom* argued. *Dad* persisted. One day, *Dad* went to work and *Mom* sledged down half the wall. When *Dad* came home, the job was done, including initial re-plastering by *Mr. Murray*. The ceiling didn't fall and the upstairs got much warmer.

Several years later, the coal stove was replaced by an oil-fired one fed from an outside tank. There was no longer a need to feed or stoke the fire, or shake it down and take out the ashes. That, to me, was luxury.

Monday was wash day, using a washer and wringer in the Oyster House, and a kerosene stove to heat water hand-pumped from the outside well. One day, we came home from school and saw that the Oyster House had burned down. Asking anything, then or later, about whether *Mom* was the cause got her dander up, producing a fierce glare that I can still recall.

Mom's food was tasty, except for store-bought canned peas in winter. I was continually scolded for not eating mine, and couldn't figure out how my brother got rid of his. *Phyllis* recently explained that he put them under the rim of his dinner plate and, when *Mom* went to the kitchen to wash dishes, *Phyllis* cleaned off the table and wiped his peas into the other table scraps (which were fed to the hogs).

Hap had another food trick. Every day, when the school bus came into view, *Mom* lined us up and shoveled a huge dose of cod liver oil into our mouths. *Phyllis* and I gulped it down. *Hap*, when we went out to catch the bus, spit his into a bush next to the porch steps. It prospered. Except for the morning glories she planted at the far end of the porch, it was the only plant I remember that thrived around *Mom*. She loved flowers, especially the Iris she called Blue Flags, and couldn't understand why hers died.

In New York, we played with a dog that looked like Tippee in the comics (Abbie & Slats). When we moved to Delaware, our parents spoke to his owners and Tippee came with us. He saw us off to school and greeted us when we returned. One day, we each had something to do after school, and none of us got off the bus. *Mom* said that Tippee, distraught, ran under the wheels of the bus and was killed. Our grief was prodigious. (*Hap* later heard about a young area man bragging about running over Tippee with his car while the dog was lying alongside the road.)

Mom fed the local dogs and strays, while telling us we couldn't have any more pets. But puppies followed *Hap* home, traveling inside his shirt when they got tired. One of those was Dottie, an unplanned cross between an Airedale and a Rat Terrier. While still a puppy, Dottie approached a rat dying from poison put out around the barn. It latched on to her nose. We knocked it off with a pole, and Dottie became a foe of rats. *Hap* and I dug out rat holes with her. When a rat came bursting out, typically going between Dottie's legs, it got about six feet away before she seized it in her jaws, shook her head mightily, crunched its bones, tossed it aside, and eagerly sought out another hole. From this I learned that dogs can remember, and hold grudges.

My brother and I put strawberries we picked on the farm in a child's wagon, pulled it to town, checked the store price, and sold ours door to door at 5¢ less (about 25¢ a quart). The people were friendly, making this decidedly unlike the treatment I later observed an African-American produce salesman undergo at John A. Tingle's store.

I once told my father that two men known for their fighting ability were very brave because they weren't afraid to fight. He disputed that, saying that real bravery required overcoming real fear.

When we went back to Philadelphia to visit the Wolfes. *Dad* and *Mom* took us to what they said was the last Horn & Hardart Automat. *Hap* and I were fascinated with the coin-operated food bins–and delighted that a lot of customers had left without taking their change. We scavenged the money, had a good meal and dessert for free, and departed with a dollar or two left over.

My father let pass no chance to extol education. Once, when we were cleaning manure out of a chicken house, I remarked on how nasty that was, there and at Eagle Poultry (where I had a summer job one year), and how there had to be a better life. *Dad* replied that, if I was serious, I needed to get an education first. In addition, he regularly barraged me with statements like:

- The man who knows how will always have a job; the man who knows why will always be the boss.

- A man's job can be taken away; his education cannot.

Dad also often harped on not giving up, saying: *It's not how many times you fall off the horse that counts, it's how many times you get back on.*

My father believed that democracy allowed everyone to do what they wanted. I said that people that free restrict the freedom of others–to the point of enslavement and murder. *Dad* settled the argument by saying that each person's freedom ends where another person's freedom begins. Thomas Jefferson expressed the same view as:

> **Rightful liberty is unobstructed action, according to our will, with limits drawn around us by the equal rights of others**.

Dad often remarked that *Man must earn his living with the sweat of his brow*. He even refused to apply for unemployment when he was without work for a long time, saying he wasn't going to be the first member of his family to take it. I remember that time from his comment the afternoon he came home, opened the refrigerator, and said: *My God, it was full this morning!* (But our meals didn't change–we charged the food at *John A. Tingle's* store until *Dad* got work.)

I worked at *John A. Tingle's* store one summer. *Dad* taught me to count from the purchase price to the amount tendered, and to not put payment in the register until change had been accepted. All went well until a man and wife paid with a $10 bill and left. The man soon returned to say that he had given me $20 but only received change for ten. *John A.* gave him $10 from the register. ($50 a week was good pay then.) The man left. The register was exactly $10 short. *John A.* said that the man was not from Frankford, had taken advantage, and wouldn't return. I was instructed to call *John A.* to oversee strangers' checkouts. But those customers didn't return, and no other payment problems arose.

Another lesson came to the store with an African-American with fresh produce to sell. He was neatly groomed, clear of eye, and articulate. Three white townsmen showed up and began asking distrustful questions. The seller answered well. *John A.* bought the produce, and the townsmen said that was OK because this was a "good nigger." He quietly took his money and left. *John A.* later bought produce from him in the back of the store. *Dad* said that *John A.* couldn't change the town, trying to do so could cause trouble, and he had treated the man fairly. I ended up respecting this African-American and with a less trusting view of the townsmen. At the time, I didn't see a threat of violence in the expectation that the "coloreds" stay in their "place." I now see this event as racial tension being handled pragmatically by *John A.* and the seller (with the townsmen unlocking Pandora's Box but not opening it). But, as such tensions escalate, the likelihood of events like the death of *Tom Bowden* increases. If fostered by hate-mongering, atrocities can result. And, when governments or large groups participate, massacres can occur (e.g., Armenia, Hitler's Germany). English novelist and scientist C. P. Snow (1905-1980) put the following perspective on this:

Civilization is hideously fragile,
there's not much between us and the Horrors underneath,
just about a coat of varnish.

My brother and I had an after-school job on a farm down Hickory Hill Road. We started upon getting off the bus, stopped when night fell, and worked all day Saturday–piling up husked corn so it could be readily shoveled into mule-drawn wagons. Our first week's pay came to about $1.50 apiece. We protested to *Dad*. He talked to the farmer and the job ended.

One summer job I held was at Green's Dairy in Millsboro. *Mr. Green* picked me up at 3:00 a.m. one day and at 3:30 a.m. the next–to alternately deliver milk to the beach and to the towns and countryside. The square glass milk bottles were easy to stack under an arm and carry–except for my sinking deeper into the beach sand. After the deliveries, we returned to the dairy to bottle milk, and I got home by 2 p.m. This seven day a week job paid $25, with *Mr. Green* buying my breakfast and, usually, lunch. I liked the job, but not the cutback in beach going.

My last high school summer job was on a State Highway Department crew that swept highway intersections except for one garbage pickup day at the beach each week. My job then was to stand in the flat-bed dump truck and empty the hot, smelly, metal garbage cans. The garbage stacked up higher than my knee-high boots, soaking me in its stench. My only enjoyment on garbage day was driving the old FWD dump truck. Nobody else wanted to because the steering wheel was so hard to turn, double-clutching the transmission produced growls of protest, and the crew's station wagon didn't smell. Coming home was unpleasant too. I had to strip in the back yard and wash off thoroughly before going into the house.

Page 55

One Sunday, I drove my brother and sister to church and skipped out–to go for a ride with our new puppy. He jumped up and licked my face. I veered across the road, hit a parked car, and my head made a hole in the windshield. The lady of the nearest house wouldn't let me in, saying I would bleed all over her new rugs. But she gave me a towel to staunch the blood and phoned for help. Seven stitches closed the wound. Being hurt, I wasn't taken to task by my parents. Later, however, I didn't stop quickly enough behind another car and broke the plastic ball decorating the center of our Studebaker's grill, and *Dad* was furious. His other upset about his sons' car use was finding the gas tank on empty in the morning–especially the time he ran out of gas before getting to the filling station less than a quarter of a mile away.

I learned about good teachers in Delaware. *Pearson Newbold Theirolf*, my high school science and home room teacher, history teacher *Mr. Walter Carmean*, and school principal *Mr. Albert Adams* all raised my opinion of their profession.

My father taught us gun safety, starting with B-B guns, before our parents gave a shotgun to *Hap* one Christmas. But *Dad* couldn't kill and wisely never owned a gun. The safe world established by those who risked their all to do so enabled him to live until he was 90. (Otherwise, he could have become one of the meek who inherit the earth early by being hastened back to it by the unrestricted strong.)

My brother oversaw our parent's last years, and saw that they had teamed up to drive because *Dad* couldn't see well enough and *Mom* couldn't turn the ignition key. *Hap* made them sell the car, and saw that they got where they needed to go.

After his eyes were failing, *Dad* listened to baseball on the radio. *Mom* didn't pay much attention, but I had learned how avid her interest was when I took them to a Phillies game. She sat next to a fan proud of knowing the city's baseball history. *Mom* was outshining him, and he reacted by asking her to name the last player to hit four home runs in a major league game in Philadelphia. She said it was Lou Gehrig and told him the date and innings. When he asked how she knew that, she answered: *I was there*. He was quiet after that.

Dad was hard-working, meticulous, puckish, and gentle. He once searched for weeks to find a 1¢ shortage in the feed store books. My idea of adding a penny to petty cash was rejected, and he found the error. As a surveyor, he was much the same, using 10-place logarithms to get the best solution. After retiring, he even did surveying problems on a hand-held calculator that he wished had been available when he was working. His last days were ones of steady weakening as his food intake dropped to virtually nothing and his body shut down.

My mother often said that those who sold liquor were doomed to Hell. (Her only drinking was a Christmas cup of eggnog.) But when my brother opened a beer and wine shop, *Mom* decided that it was sellers of hard liquor who were doomed. Medicinal use of alcohol was OK though. She gave me a "hot flip" a few times when I was coughing too much to sleep. Its hot water laced with whiskey worked.

Mom was our disciplinarian and, consistent with her upbringing, could be harsh about it. But she rejected hatred, teaching that it destroys those who hate. Over time, she mellowed, caring deeply for her grandchildren and leaving them all bequests in her will. After *Dad* died, *Mom* slept on her half of their bed just as if he were still on the other side. She passed on a few months later, the night before she was to be taken to a nursing home because her irascibility had made her hired care givers stop coming. *Mom* had long feared and railed against nursing homes, and we're not sure if she knew that was coming.

The following chart my own family and those of my brother and sister.

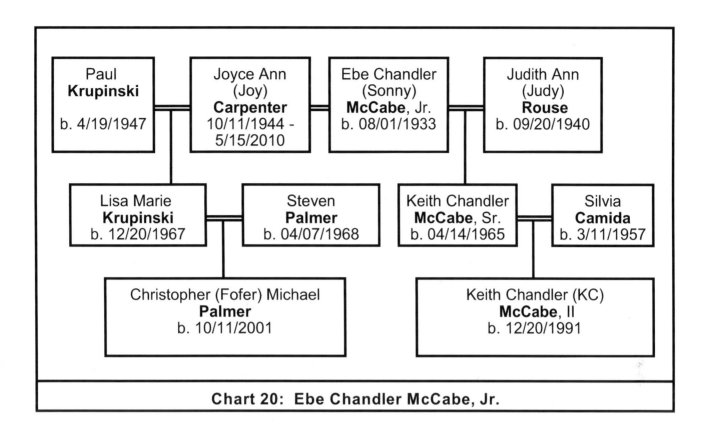

Chart 20: Ebe Chandler McCabe, Jr.

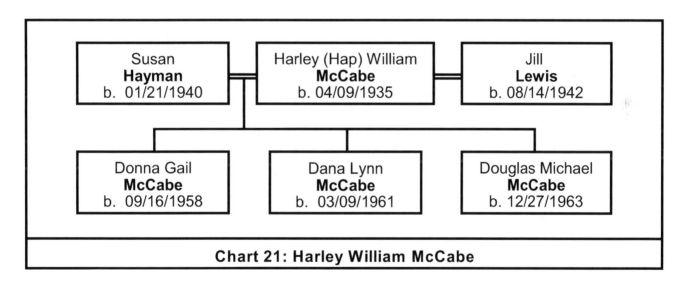

Chart 21: Harley William McCabe

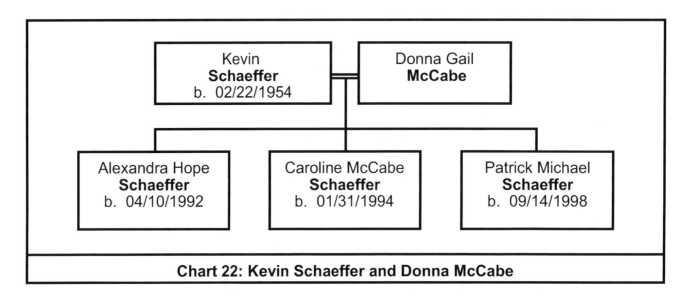

Chart 22: Kevin Schaeffer and Donna McCabe

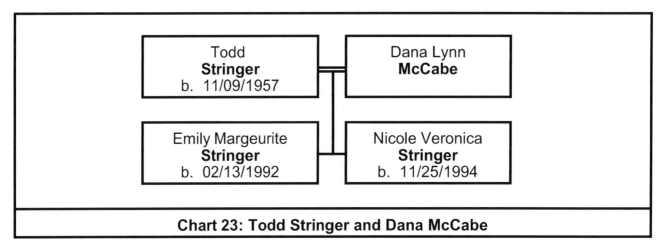

Chart 23: Todd Stringer and Dana McCabe

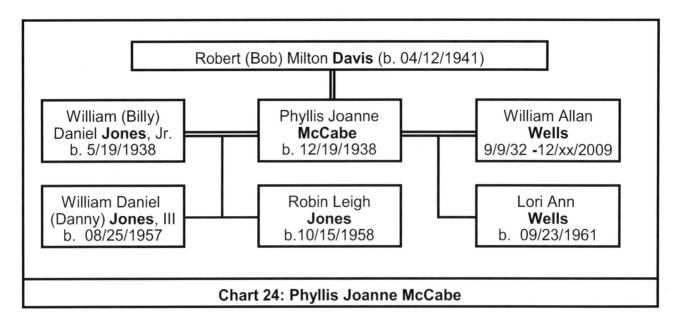

Chart 24: Phyllis Joanne McCabe

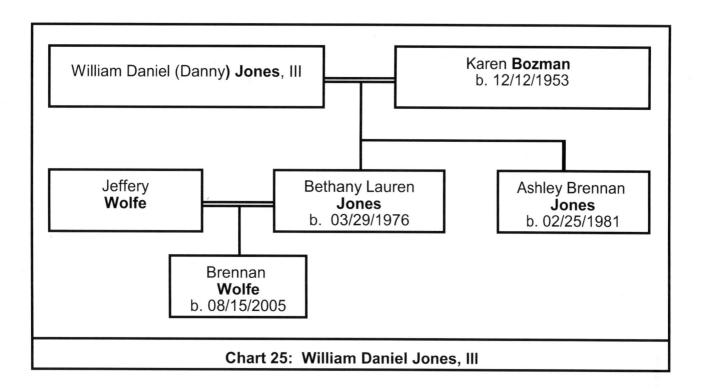

Chart 25: William Daniel Jones, III

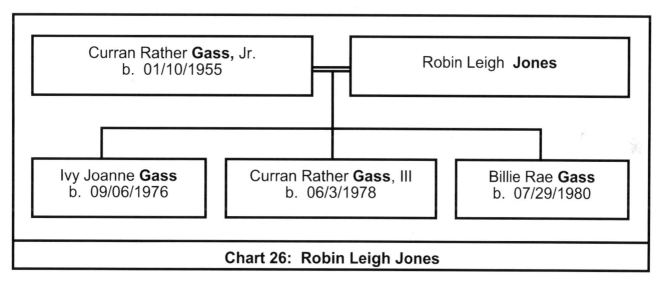

Chart 26: Robin Leigh Jones

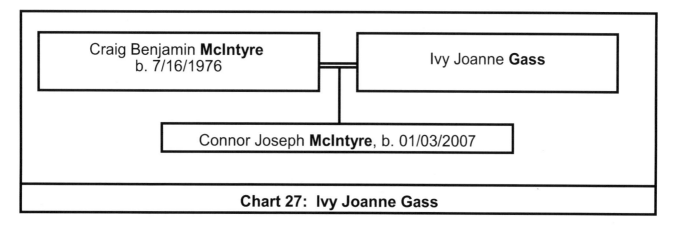

Chart 27: Ivy Joanne Gass

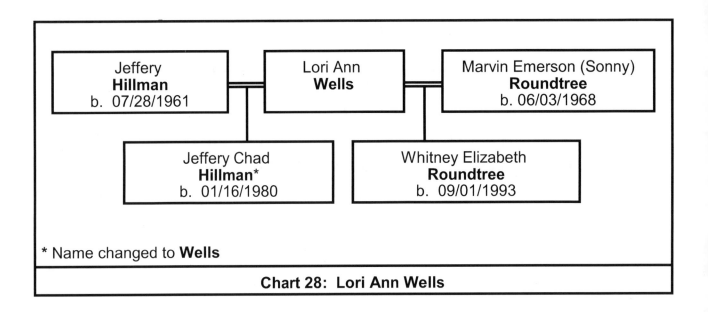

* Name changed to **Wells**

Chart 28: Lori Ann Wells

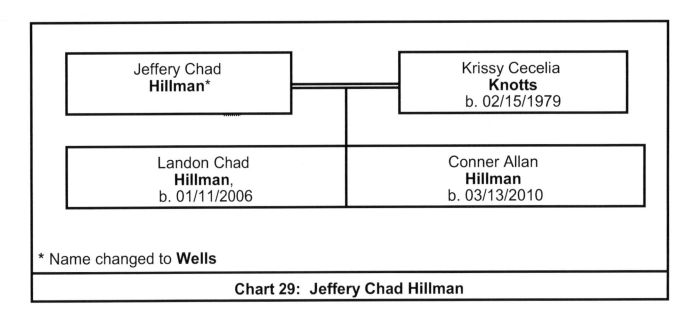

* Name changed to **Wells**

Chart 29: Jeffery Chad Hillman

The Coulis (Kulas) Family

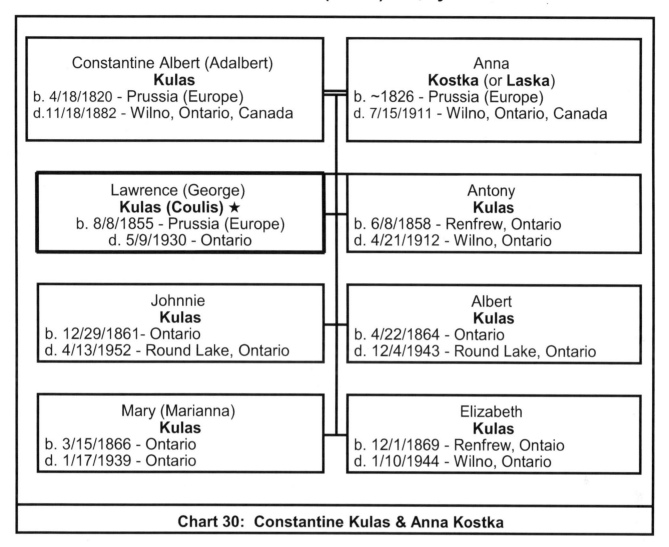

Constantine Albert (Adalbert) **Kulas** b. 4/18/1820 - Prussia (Europe) d. 11/18/1882 - Wilno, Ontario, Canada	Anna **Kostka** (or **Laska**) b. ~1826 - Prussia (Europe) d. 7/15/1911 - Wilno, Ontario, Canada
Lawrence (George) **Kulas (Coulis)** ★ b. 8/8/1855 - Prussia (Europe) d. 5/9/1930 - Ontario	Antony **Kulas** b. 6/8/1858 - Renfrew, Ontario d. 4/21/1912 - Wilno, Ontario
Johnnie **Kulas** b. 12/29/1861- Ontario d. 4/13/1952 - Round Lake, Ontario	Albert **Kulas** b. 4/22/1864 - Ontario d. 12/4/1943 - Round Lake, Ontario
Mary (Marianna) **Kulas** b. 3/15/1866 - Ontario d. 1/17/1939 - Ontario	Elizabeth **Kulas** b. 12/1/1869 - Renfrew, Ontaio d. 1/10/1944 - Wilno, Ontario

Chart 30: Constantine Kulas & Anna Kostka

Mom's ancestors were Polish. Poles are descended from the West Slavic tribes of West Prussia. Pagan Germans (Prussians) invaded and settled there in the 7th Century. The Teutonic knights, a military religious order, conquered Prussia in 1226.[153]

In the late 19th Century, West Prussia was bounded by the Baltic Sea (to the north), by East Prussia, by Poland and the Grand Duchy of Poznan (to the south), and by Brandenburg and Pomerania (to the west). In 1883, 13,749 people left West Prussia to emigrate to America. Others left to seek work in Westphalia and Saxony, and there was expulsion of Poles who weren't naturalized Prussians. By 1887, ~29,000 of the estimated total of over 500,000 Poles[154] had departed.

In 1900, East Prussia was bounded by the Baltic (northwest), Russia (northeast) Poland (east and south), and West Prussia. In 1800, the primary language was German, with a Polish-speaking minority in the southeast.[155]

Pre-WWI Eastern Europe held the Austro-Hungarian Empire, the German Empire (East Prussia, Posen, Silesia, West Prussia), the Russian Empire (including Poland), and Romania.[156] So my Polish ancestors lived in the German Empire, with linkage to the Russian Empire seeming likely.

Besides *Coulis*, *Kulas* name variations include *Kolis* (the spelling on *Mom's* birth certificate), *Kulis*, *Klaus*, *Kloss*, *Koilas*, and others. One reference[157] considers the name source to be the ancient Greek name *Nikolaos*, meaning the conquering people. *Fred Hoffman*, the author of *Polish Surnames, Origins and Meanings*, considers that plausible,[158] but notes several potential sources (See Appendix 1). He noted[159] that most names from *kul-* basically mean "cripple" (from the meaning of "crutch" for *Kula*). So the leg deformity *Mom* thought her father got from a wood-chopping accident may have been inherited.

Constantine and *Anna* settled in Wilno, the first Polish settlement in Canada. Wilno is close to the Ontario-Quebec border, west of Ottawa, near Algonquin Provincial Park, about 285 road miles from Niagara Falls. It's in Renfrew County. Cobalt, where the family moved, is about 260 road miles northwest of Wilno.

Johnnie Kulas, a son of *Constantine* and *Anna*, had the following offspring.

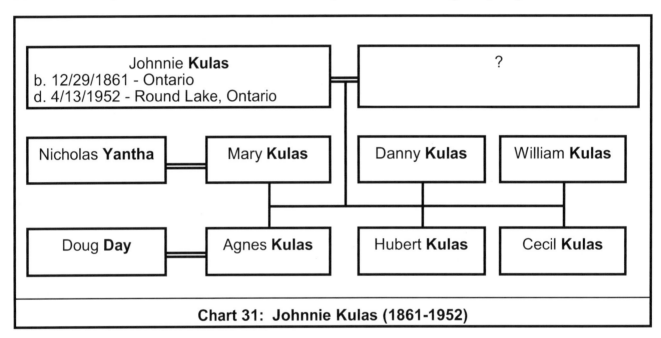

Chart 31: Johnnie Kulas (1861-1952)

My maternal grandfather took the surname *Coulis* about 1891, before moving to Cobalt. *Mom* seldom spoke of her parents. She did say that she and her mother hadn't gotten along. She also spoke of walking, alone, to her father's cabin in the woods, being terrified by the howling of the wolves, and not going there again. *Mom* seldom saw her siblings, though she was very fond of them and often wrote.

Bob Pascoe said that our grandfather was a hunter/trapper who came home once a year to beat up his family and sire another baby. His first four children didn't survive long. The next seven emigrated to the United States, with the earlier arrivals helping the others. Their family tree follows.

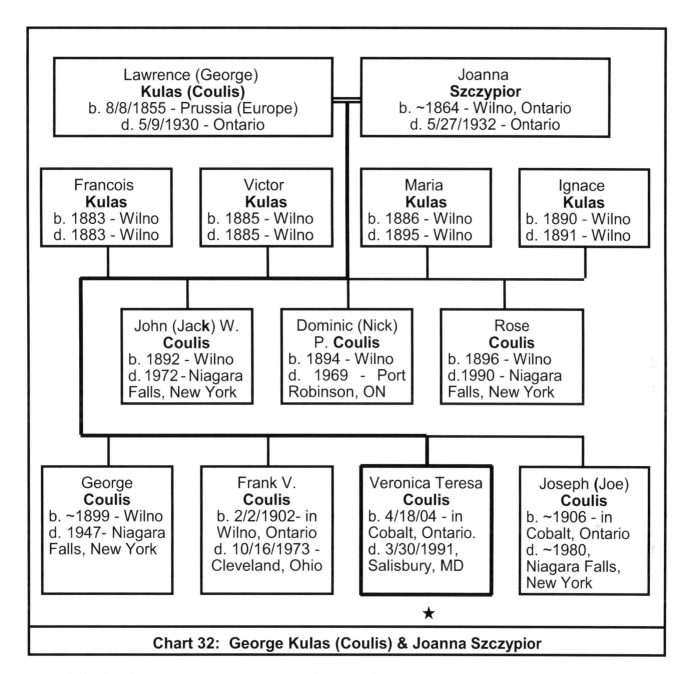

Chart 32: George Kulas (Coulis) & Joanna Szczypior

I recall visiting *Uncle Joe* and enjoying his family. *Uncle Frank* I remember for his punishing me by pulling my hair. That hurt, but my parents weren't at all put out.

Uncle Jack, his siblings' father figure, was a tough miner, lumberjack, and steeplejack. In his 70s he was jailed for fighting over union matters with a man under 30. *Uncle Jack* was also caring. He saw his farmer brother *Nick* whipping his horses, took the whip, and said he'd use it on *Nick* if he saw him doing that again. When *Uncle Jack* visited *Mom* after retiring, there were boxes of partially empty liquor bottles in the attic–ones I'd left during moves. *She* asked if he could have some. I said sure and, to her discomfiture but not mine, he drank it all.

Uncle George was our favorite uncle. When he visited us in New York, he gave both *Hap* and me a two-holster set of Dick Tracy cap pistols, saw that we weren't enthused, and dug the why out of us over *Mom's* protests. Dick Tracy used one gun in a shoulder holster, and we liked

Gene Autry. So *Uncle George* replaced the toys with two, two-holster Gene Autry cap pistol sets that we were delighted to have.

Uncle George took my brother and me to a saloon—once. Until then, we had no idea what one was. This one had a long, polished wooden bar. We sat next to our uncle and drank ginger ale. He had beer. The bartender slid our drinks to us from way down the bar, and our glasses stopped right in front of each of us. We told Mom that. She turned on her brother with: YOU TOOK **MY** CHILDREN INTO A BAR!!! He was deep in the doghouse for a while.

Dad and *Uncle George* once returned from a baseball game tipsily singing *My Gal Sal.* Mom was embarrassed. But she blamed her brother's drinking on his girl friend *Gert*, and felt that he just needed to marry someone nice. (*Hap* remembers *Gert* as being nice.) *Uncle George* died from cirrhosis—destitute, alcoholic, and beyond help. His siblings didn't give him money because it only went to drink.

We did get to know several of *Aunt Rose's* children. Their family tree follows.

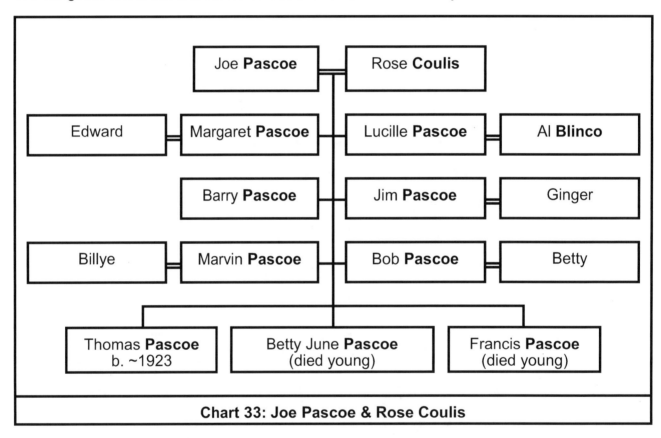

Chart 33: Joe Pascoe & Rose Coulis

Lucille secretly married *Al Blinco*, a U.S. Navy sailor, and confided that to her mother when she became pregnant. *Aunt Rose,* afraid of what *Lucille's* father would do, sent her to live with us. She had a huge appetite during her pregnancy. Mom once fried (in Crisco) chicken just for *Lucille* and me, stopping after we ate six birds. (*George Murray* had sold his current crop of chickens. That always resulted in some heads getting crushed. Those birds were quickly decapitated and hung to drain, and everyone around then had a lot of chicken to eat.)

Al left the Navy before *Lucille* gave birth, and took her to Hollywood, Florida. I saw them once more, when I was living in Ohio with my own family. After putting their kids through college while owning a swimming pool cleaning business, *Al* became an Amway distributor. He was driving a Mercedes, recruiting, and deploring how most people worked for too little pay and a "dead turkey" for Christmas–while Amway let everyone advance as far as they could. (I remember his description of the company as giving each recruiter a cut of the sales of his or her recruits, and their's, etc.) I wasn't interested. Neither, I think, was anyone else in the family, except that *Lucille's* brother *Barry* may have tried it for awhile.

Lucille died years ago. I haven't met her children. *Bob Pascoe* told me that her firstborn, *Sharon*, read him the names in a phone book when she was three, and that she graduated 1st of ~1000 in her Syracuse University class. Sharon married a Jordanian. They initially settled overseas and are now back in the United States, where he works at the World Bank.

Jim Pascoe became a gregarious, successful businessman who owned a heavy construction equipment rental business and a limousine rental service. My brother visited him several times, and received a limousine tour on each visit. There were flags on the front fenders (mounted like those on dignitary-carrying limos). One flag was American, the other Polish. No one noticed the Polish one.

Marvin and Bob Pascoe and I (and my then eight-year-old son *Keith*) went fishing for walleye in Canada, up past Sault Ste. Marie on a lake near a several thousand acre farm *Marvin* had bought, for $2/acre, as a retirement investment. It was at the end of the electric line, lay fallow, and had several vacant farmhouses. *Keith* caught his first fish that week. I also met a group of my Canadian relatives then. The first night we partied, and decided to go fishing early. In the morning, an alarm went off. Someone groggily said: *It's six o'clock!* Another voice said: *Yes, the Little Hand is on the Six and the Big Hand is on the Twelve.* Quiet then reigned until we all went fishing at noon. That weekend ended too quickly–my new-found relatives had to work on Monday. But *Bob, Marvin, Keith* and I enjoyed fishing for the rest of the week.

I thoroughly enjoyed *Bob, Jim,* and *Marvin. Jim* quoted "Polish" proverbs (e.g., the Golden Rule: the man who has the gold makes the rules). *Bob* described his Navy hitch in minesweepers as involving more brig than sea time. *Marvin* once, to his wife's and mother's horror, answered a Canadian Border Guard's question about their purpose in visiting Canada (while Queen Elizabeth was there) by saying that it was to assassinate the Queen (getting only a dressing down from the guard, who may have shared *Marvin's* perspective).

I regret not knowing my Polish family better.

Genetic Roots

Growing up in rural Delaware identified no unique Irish or Scottish or British or Welsh ethos. There were many Democrats, few Republicans, devout and Sunday Présbyterians and Methodists, and local loyalties. It was a community of cultural cousins without Old World ethnicity being evident. That's the effect of the American melting pot. But we do look at our ancestral lineage in terms of its geographic and genetic origins.

This history began with the customary, patrilineal (surname) approach to the descendants of *Captain Joshua L. Chandler* and *John S. McCabe (1727-1800).* That gave an incomplete picture. Each of us is descended from a mother too, and they contribute a lot (often most) to a child's upbringing. As lawyer, poet and songwriter William Ross Wallace (1819-1881) put it:

For the hand that rocks the cradle–Is the hand that rules the world.

Also, maternal ancestry counts as much as paternal ancestry. For example, my stepdaughter's father is Polish (as is my mother). And, her mother's mother was a lower Delaware woman with the Irish maiden name Cannon, while my father was a lower Delaware man with the Irish-Scotch-Irish name McCabe. So, despite the differences indicated by my stepdaughter being born a Krupinski and me being born a McCabe, we really have very similar heritages. The same is true of many people. Marriage intermingles and mixes behavioral characteristics to produce the culture one grows up in. It can make one's culture more representative of blended ancestry than that of either parent, the common characteristics of close relatives notwithstanding. So, to get a better overall perspective on my family's wider genetic and cultural background, I looked at maternal surnames from my father's family, from my mother's family, from my high school classmates, and from people I knew in Delaware. They show (Appendix 1) rural Delaware's intermingled English, Scotch, Irish, Welsh, Norman and Germanic roots.

Vernon McCabe's work relates tales that *1727 John McCabe's* father was a doctor in Belfast, and that his ancestors were cattle drovers in the Scottish Highlands. So far, those roots are unconfirmed. But we can trace our ancestry past specific parental information by using the work of Brian Sykes,[160] Professor of Human Genetics at the University of Oxford. Myth and historic data (including surnames) contribute to Dr. Sykes' conclusions, but his work is based on DNA analysis. It shows, from over 10,000 DNA samples taken in the Isles (i.e., Ireland and Britain), a closely related ancestry.

The ancestry Sykes traced dates back to the Upper Paleolithic and Mesolithic settlers who reached the Isles about 8000 BC. The Upper Paleolithic was the last phase of the Old Stone Age. It lasted until the end of the last ice age (~11,000 BC). A later cold phase (the Younger Dryas) brought the ice back from ~9000 BC to ~8000 BC and cleared the Isles of human settlers (except perhaps in Southern England). The Mesolithic Era lasted from then to the Neolithic (farming) Era, which began in Europe ~6500 BC and spread to the Isles ~4000 BC.[161]

Stone Age hunter-gatherers have been depicted as unintelligent "cave men." But our hunter-gatherer ancestors may have been smarter than we are. Their hand-to-mouth lives depended on adaptability, resourcefulness, and a broad range of knowledge. When agriculture fostered a huge population increase, individuals who could not survive and reproduce as hunter-gatherers may have become more likely to do so as specialists. Jared Diamond, a Pulitzer Prize-winning Professor of Geography at the University of California, Los Angeles reached a related conclusion. His perception was that intelligence was ruthlessly selected for in New Guinea's hunter-gatherers because war, murder, and starvation were their primary causes of death. Diamond also hypothesized that natural selection in densely populated regions favors those more resistant to disease.[162] (A supporting fact is that, early in the Civil War, childhood diseases like measles killed a lot of Union and Confederate soldiers from rural areas.[163])

Sykes used Y Chromosome DNA (Y-DNA) to trace the male descent of the people of Ireland and Britain. Men have one Y Chromosome and one X Chromosome. It's the Y Chromosome that makes them male. (Women have two X Chromosomes and no Y Chromosome.) So sons, their father, and that father's father, etc., have the same Y-DNA as well as the same surname. (Surname histories and Y-DNA histories both trace patrilineal ancestry.)

Mitochondrial DNA (mtDNA) shows the direct female (matrilineal) descent of individuals. Its evidence lies in the energy-providing mitochondria in human cells. The mitochondria of sperm fuel their journey to the egg, but are discarded upon impregnation. So mtDNA is inherited only from the mother, and from her mother, and hers, etc. It defines matrilineal ancestry in the same way that surnames and Y Chromosome DNA define patrilineal lineage.

If DNA did not change, everyone's would be alike, except for the sex difference. But DNA changes (mutations) occur and are inherited. They produce a DNA signature specific to their origin. When a populace migrates, its mutations can be used to trace the path back to their geographic origin. The mutation rates are used to approximate the chronology of the migration.

Professor Sykes found that the matrilineal lineages of the Isles are ancient and continuous, go back to the original settlers, and are most closely related to the matrilineal lineages of Western and Northern Iberia (Spain and Portugal). He hypothesized that the main Neolithic settlers of the Isles came, via the Iberian route, as family-based units. Many Irish Celts, male and female, arrived there when farming did. By ~4000 BC, maternal migration established the Isles' present matrilineal lineage, which is basically unchanged and represents the Isles' Celtic stock. The Scottish Picts, once thought to be genetically different, also are of the same basic stock. Matrilineally, almost all the Isles' inhabitants are Celts.

There *are* some matrilineal differences. The Northern Isles (Orkney and Shetland) have a matrilineal link to Norway, indicating that as many Norse women as men migrated there. And, ~40% of Shetlanders and ~30% of Orcadians have Viking ancestry.[164] Also, European farming began in the fertile crescent east of the Mediterranean Sea,[165] spread west and overland to the Baltic and the North Sea, and coastally to Iberia and the French Coast. Coastal route DNA is found throughout the Isles; overland route DNA is found only on Britain's east side, in small numbers. A third, tiny group in Southern England has a maternal link to sub-Saharan Africa (two women) and to Syria or Jordan (three women). These may be descendants of Roman slaves, indicating that the Roman matrilineal effect was minute. Sykes found one unattributable African sequence in Stornway in the Western Isles,[166] and his data very consistently shows the Celtic matrilineal character of virtually all of the Isles' inhabitants.

On the male side, Celtic ancestry linked to Iberia also predominates in the Isles, with clusters of specific Y-DNA variants. In mid-Wales and parts of Scottish "Pictland," the variants indicate forebearers among the first Mesolithic settlers, who may have walked to the Isles before the melting ice separated Ireland and Britain from the mainland. Y Chromosomes characteristic of the Irish Ui Nèill Clan (who forced Dal Riata Clan emigration to Scotland) are most common in northwest Ireland. Another Y Chromosome variant, common in the Hebrides and the Highlands, is significant elsewhere only in descendants of Clans Donald and Dougall. The patrilineal lineage of the Isles is less diverse than the matrilineal lineage: there are five main groups of Y Chromosomes and thirteen main groups of mitochondria.[167]

Sykes attributed the Y-DNA clusters to the "Genghis effect," named for Genghis Khan's practice of killing the men in conquered lands and impregnating the attractive women. In those times, the longer a closely related group of men held power, the more similar the region's Y-DNA became.[168]

Normans, Saxons and Danes are genetically similar. Because of the scarcity of Norman surnames, Sykes estimated the overall patrilineal Norman lineage at 2% or less–even in South England. He estimated that ~10% of the men in South England are patrilineally descended from Saxons or Danes. Above the Danelaw line (from London northwest to the coast near Liverpool), that rises to 15%, peaking at 20% in East Anglia. The Saxon/Dane invasions did produce a local Y-DNA incidence about double that of their mtDNA counterpart, indicating that some displacement of indigenous males took place. But there are still far more Celtic descendants than Danish/Saxon ones in every part of England.[169]

Sykes found a rare potential patrilineal link to the Romans in England. Recruitment of legionnaires and auxiliaries from Gaul (France), Britannia, and elsewhere may be a reason for the lack of genetic evidence of the Roman occupation.

Sykes' data comes from tiny, non-functional (in known inherited characteristics) parts of the human genome, not on any of the ~10,000 genes (by Sykes count) that determine our genetically inherited traits. So Sykes' data does not support drawing individual or group conclusions about inherited diseases, intelligence, appearance, athleticism, strength, etc.

Another consideration is that we each have two parents, four grandparents, eight great-great grandparents, etc. Each generation of our ancestors contains twice as many individuals as the generation that follows it. Some of our ancestors appear more than once in our lineage, but tracing our ancestral tree back more than ~500 years still shows that we have more ancestors than genes, meaning that some of our ancestors who lived before ~1500 AD did not contribute a whole gene to our genomes.[170] Even tracing our ancestry back beyond a few generations presents a genetic mixing that we cannot unscramble.

The fact that the basic Celtic stock of Ireland and Britain hasn't changed indicates that the DNA Sykes found to be predominantly Celtic was accompanied by a corresponding predominance of bisexually inherited Celtic genes. That doesn't mean that local and regional and even national traits of Ireland and Britain aren't a result of both Celtic and non-Celtic genes. For example, in the Hebrides, the Northern Islands, the coastal areas between Ireland and Scotland, and along the English Channel, there were substantive Viking incursions. Consequently, some reproductively advantageous Viking genes must have been inserted into the indigenous genomes of the time. It seems inevitable that some of those non-indigenous genes proliferated in some areas of Ireland and Britain, and even throughout those Isles in some cases, and from there came to the Americas.[171]

My Y-DNA indicates an ~70% probability that my fifth cousin, *Vernon McCabe*, and I have a common ancestor within six generations.[172] From *Vernon's* work, we know that we are both 6th generation descendants of *1727 John McCabe*. And, our DNA extends our ancestry back past Ireland and Scotland to a male ancestor who lived on the Iberian Peninsula about 25 thousand years ago (25 KYA).[173] Professor Sykes named him Oisin (pronounced Osheen).[174] He was the progenitor of the haplogroup titled R1b, believed to be descended from the first modern humans to enter Europe–about 35-40 KYA. Their descendants made the cave paintings in France and Spain.[175] Oisin's became the most common European Y-DNA haplogroup, and expanded throughout Mainland Europe (and to Ireland and Britain) after the last ice age.[176] Most of his descendants (including my patrilineal family) are in the R1b1 subset. A partial list of the Sykes-apportioned percentage of the R1b1 men of some specific ethnicities follows.[177]

Wales	83%	Ireland	80%
Scotland	72%	England	64%
Basques	90%	Poland	75%
Punjab	60%	Greece	35%
Uzbekistan	30%	the Maori	30%

In my case, Oisin's matrilineal counterpart is Helena. Her progeny comprise about 45.6% of the Irish populace.[178] Clan Helena also makes up 45.3% of Scotland's people, 45.7 % of Wales' population, and 45.7% of England's inhabitants.[179] Helena was born in Southern France, about 20 KYA, during the Last Glacial Maximum. Her people's habitat included the Dordogne River Valley and extended eastward to the Gulf of Lion on the Mediterranean Sea and westward to the Bay of Biscay region of the Atlantic Ocean.[180] After the ice retreated, Helena's daughters became the most populous mtDNA Haplogroup in Western Europe. They migrated eastward too, where my mother's deeper ancestry lies.

Dr. Sykes placed Oisin's birthplace as south of the Pyrenees Mountains, with Helena's to their north. Different human groups, including races, have genomes that are 99.9% similar. Of the 0.1% difference, 0.0854% is within populations, 0.0083% is between similar groups (like Greeks and Swedes), and the other 0.0063% is between races.[181] So ethnicity can have been the primary difference between Oisin's clan and Helena's.

Oisin and Helena are descended, respectively, from the patrilineal and matrilineal Most Recent Common Ancestors (MRCAs) of us all. Those MRCAs were not the first human male and female, or even contemporaries. The mates with whom they established their lineages are not traceable because of the complexity of bisexual inheritance. (Appendix 5 provides some insight into genetic drift and other factors that caused our lines to survive and other lines to die out.)

The following charts trace my family's deep ancestry from Clans Oisin and Helena back to their Y-MRCA and mtMRCA.[182]

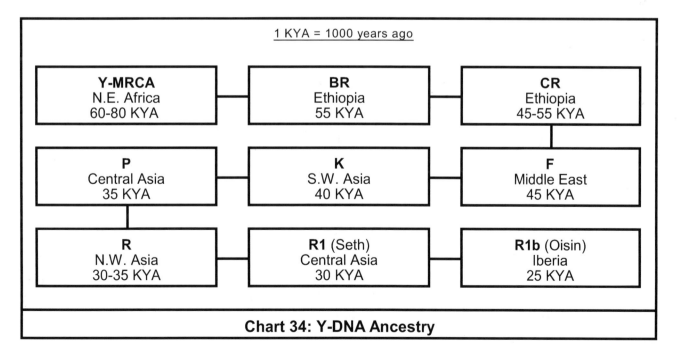

Chart 34: Y-DNA Ancestry

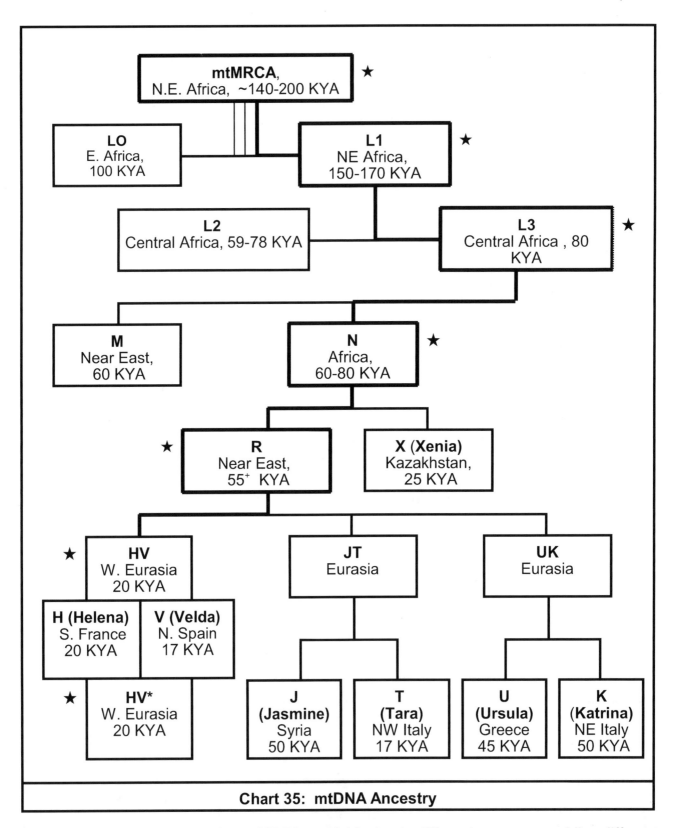

Chart 35: mtDNA Ancestry

Note: The overlap between the mtMRCA and L1 is due to different sources providing different dates, but L1 is typically shown as an mtMRCA descendant. Inability to clearly discriminate between potential pathways led to clumping of the HV and HV* pathway.

Genetic Term Glossary

Autosomes
Chromosomes other than the X and Y (sex determining) Chromosomes.

Chromosome
A strand of DNA containing specific genes. The chromosomes are located within the nucleus of each cell. Our species has 23 pairs of chromosomes that together hold about 10,000 genes. (Some sources say there are 20,000-30,000 genes in our DNA. So gene definition and counting methodology isn't uniform, or hasn't been for very long.)

DNA
Deoxyribonucleic acid: molecular strands of genetic material (nucleic acids) that prescribe inherited characteristics of life forms on Earth.

Gene
A DNA sequence that makes up a unit of heredity. Genes encode specific amino acids and proteins. They are carried on chromosomes and in mitochondria. (Gene is the name later given to the unit of heredity that Gregor Mendel called a "factor.")

Haplogroup
The set of all Male (or of all female) descendants of the person who first showed a sequence variation for one of the four nucleotides (Adenine, Thymine, Cytosine, and Guanine) that make up DNA sequences.

Haplotype
A set of genes, close together on a chromosome, that tend to be inherited together.

Matrilineal
The line of descent through the mother, and through that mother's mother, and through that mother's mother's mother, etc. (Men are not in the matrilineal line of descent.)

Mitochondria
Organelles in each cell. Mitochondria reside in a cell's cytoplasm, which is outside the cell nucleus. They have their own DNA, which contains less than 40 genes. The mitochondria transform nutrients into the energy that fuels their cells.

Mutation
A change in a cell characteristic. Mutations result from inexact transcription of DNA during production and replication. Somatic mutations affect the individual only; reproductive cell mutations are inherited by subsequent generations. Most mutations are harmful and have little chance of propagating. Some mutations are neutral; these are potentially useful in identifying relatedness of individuals and groups. A few mutations are beneficial and likely to increase in incidence by providing a reproductive advantage.

Patrilineal
The male line of descent through the father, and through his father's father, and through his father's father's father, etc. (Women are not in the patrilineal line of descent.)

Somatic Cells
Body Cells other than the reproductive ones.

Myth-Generated Culture

Human culture has always had mythic inputs. *Brigadoon*, a 1947 Broadway show, retold a very old German tale about the mythical village of Gemelhausen, which appeared for one day every 100 years, as a Scottish love story.[183] *Camelot*, a 1960 Broadway show, retold the tale of King Arthur and Lancelot and Guenevere and the Knights of the Round Table in the setting of a magical utopia.[184] Both stories show how authors insert their own spin into mythical tales. *Brigadoon* also showed the multi-ethnic nature of myth, and *Camelot* became a part of American culture through its association with the Kennedy (JFK) administration.[185]

President Kennedy's 1000 day presidency represented my then young generation's mistaken belief that he and his lovely wife Jacqueline would lead us into a new era of peace and prosperity, correcting earlier generations' errors. Its public link to *Camelot* occurred soon after JFK's November 1963 funeral, when Jacqueline Kennedy invited Theodore White to interview her for an article on JFK. (It was published in the December 6, 1963 edition of Life Magazine.) Mrs. Kennedy spoke of playing the final song of *Camelot* repeatedly for her husband, and of his view that history was full of heroes. For JFK, those who worked for social justice and enrichment of people's lives were counterparts of the Knights of the Round Table. Landmarks of his presidency included starting the Peace Corps, a failed American attempt to invade Cuba, and facing down the USSR to get Russian missiles out of Cuba. But the youthful JFK wasn't able to get Congress to follow his lead, and the Civil Rights legislation he wanted was enacted because of the acumen of his much older successor, Lyndon Baines Johnson.

Religion and myth and art sometimes combine to contribute to our culture. For example:

> *My heart leaps up when I behold*
> *A rainbow in the sky:*
> *So was it when my life began;*
> *So is it now I am a man;*
> *So be it when I shall grow old,*
> *Or let me die!*
> *The Child is father of the Man;*
> *I could wish my days to be*
> *Bound each to each by natural piety.*

The above 1802 William Wordsworth poem linked rainbows[186] to piety in childhood, adulthood, and old age, using the role of rainbows before and since God promised Noah the world would not be again destroyed by flood. And, the well-known phrase about the child being father to the man recognizes childhood's learning carryover into adulthood.

Religion's, myth's, and art's combined role also is shown in an Auld Scottish Prayer:

> *From ghoulies and ghosties,*
> *And long-leggedy beasties,*
> *And things that go bump in the night,*
> *Dear Lord, deliver us.*

That prayer illustrates how pre-Christian beliefs were incorporated into our culture and religion. Many people fear ghosts, but there are no ghosts in the Christian religion, and the ghoul is a mythical monster from ancient Arabian folklore.[187]

Halloween, initially a Celtic holiday, has origins in the harvest festival of Samhein. It came to America in the culture and religion of Irish and Scotch immigrants,[188] and persists in our own. Parts of it have been incorporated into Christianity's All Saints Day. Some aspects have become primarily a children's celebration.

Before Celtic written language was developed in the 7th Century AD, Celtic history was passed down by word of mouth that inevitably incorporated tale-tellers' poetic license and fantasies.[189] Ireland has held on so staunchly to its Celtic culture that its surviving folklore, including leprechauns and the pot of gold at the end of the rainbow, is particularly handy for delving into the Celtic pre-Christian character.

The legend of the *Tuatha Dé Danaan* (people of the Goddess Dana) has been said to have so strong a hold on the Irish that it was not shaken from their minds by Christianity.[190] These *Tuatha* were among Ireland's mythical initial settlers and were believed to have superhuman powers, including "majick," but to be less than Gods.[191] A taste of their saga follows.

Ireland's first inhabitants were:

- *Fintann* and *Cesair* (his wife), and 16 women.

- *Bith* (*Cesair's* father) and *Bairrfind* (*Cesair's* companion), and 16 women;

- *Ladra*, the vessel's pilot, and 16 women.

Ladra died, supposedly of too many women. So *Fintann* and *Bith* each took eight of *Ladra's* women, whereupon *Bith* went north and died. *Fintann* then escaped from all the women, morphed into a salmon, and lived for a year in the waters in a cave named "Fintann's Grave" above Tul Tinde (the Hill of the Wave). He then became other creatures, living for thousands of years. *Cesair*, with her father dead and husband gone, died of heartbreak.

Ireland's next settlers were the *Partholonians*. They came from the west, beyond the Atlantic, perhaps from "Greek Scythia" (which may mean the Other World of Faerie). *Partholon*, after reputedly killing his parents in a futile try to gain their chiefdom, led his followers to what is now Munster. There they found people with a leader who reportedly came from the Caucasus. Those people either left Ireland or were assimilated by the *Partholonians*.

The *Partholonians* were superb at brewing, cauldron making, and combat. Known as shapers of the land, they added to Ireland's initial three lakes, nine rivers, and one plain, and are credited with being Ireland's first farmers and with creating and naming places in Ireland.

While *Partholon* was away hunting and fishing, his wife *Dealgnaid* slept with his servant. In Ireland's first jealous rage, *Partholon* then killed his wife's lapdog. *Dealgnaid* asserted that her infidelity was due to her husband leaving her alone, and *Partholon* accepted that. That blame, titled *The Right of his Wife Against Partholon*, was said to be the first judgement in Ireland.

Partholon and *Dealgnaid* had three sons, *Eber* (the eldest), *Rudraihe*, and *Laighllinne*. They also had six "pure" daughters, indicating that *Partholon* (and/or *Dealgnaid*) may have had "impure" children too–perhaps outside their marriage. The *Partholonians* battled with the *Fomorii*, who were sea-raiders. Tory Island, off the coast of Donegal, was the *Fomorian* stronghold. The *Fomorii* were described as ugly, one-eyed, one-legged, or one-armed beings from *Fomoria*, which may be Scandinavia. They were believed to be from the underworld and to represent Chaos and Destruction.

In their third century in Ireland, plague killed all but a few of the more than 9000 *Partholonians*. About 30 years later, *Partholonian* history ended. *Tuan MacStarn*, the son of *Partholon's* brother *Starn*, survived the demise of his people. He wandered the vacant land, seeking shelter from wolves, until he morphed into a young stag and lived to an old age as Ireland's King of Stags. *Tuan* then became a young boar that lived to old age, and repeated the sequence as an eagle.

He eventually changed into a salmon that was caught and eaten by *Cairell's* wife, who gave birth to *Tuan* in human form. This *Tuan MacCairell* knew his history and that of Ireland beginning with the *Partholonians*. He related it all to Christian monks, who recorded it.

Tuan told the monks that, after wandering for many years, he saw, from a high hill, *Nemed MacAgnoman* take possession of Ireland. (Before becoming a stag, *Tuan* was "long haired, clawed, decrepit, naked, wretched, and miserable," and that made him avoid the *Nemedians*.) *Nemed* (whose name means sacred) was the leader of Greek Scythians related to the *Partholonians*. They sailed from their homeland in 34 ships, each ship carrying 30 people. In the Atlantic Ocean, a golden tower appeared when the tide was low. To get the gold, the *Nemedians* steered toward the tower, foundered on shoals, and lost most of their ships and people. The survivors included *Nemed*, his four chieftain sons, and their wives. They wandered the ocean for a year and half in the ships they had left. Those few who did not die of hunger and thirst reached Ireland.

The *Nemedians* also were raided by the *Fomorii*, who took children, corn,[192] and milk from them as tribute. After many years of that, the *Nemedians* attacked the *Fomorii* on Tory Island, killing the *Fomorian* leader. *Fomorian* reinforcements arrived and all but 30 *Nemedians* were killed. *Chief Britan* led some of the escaping *Nemedians* to Britain. The others, after much wandering, returned to Ireland at about the same time as did the *Firbolg* and the *Tuatha Dé Danaan*.

The first *Firbolg* tribe was the *Euerni*, called *Erainn*. They named the new land *Eueriio*, which became *Eriu,* then *Éire* in Old Irish, and then Ireland. These *Nemedians* had been enslaved for more than 300 years in Greece, where they carried lowland clay in bags to manure lands higher up, gaining the name *Firbolg* (men of bags). They kept alive the stories of their ancestors' green island. About 5000 of them escaped in stolen Greek ships, landed at Blackrod Bay in northwest Ireland (now in County Mayo), and established a chiefdom centered on Tara. Except for *Fomorian* raids, they held sway in Ireland for 37 years.

In the tenth year of the reign of *Eochaidh*, Chief of the Firbolg, the *Tuatha* challenged the *Firbolg* for supremacy, and offered to split Ireland between the two tribes. The *Firbolg* preferred war, but saw that their opposition was better armed and asked for time to make better weapons. The *Tuatha* agreed. The matter was settled at the first battle of Magh Tuiredh (Montura, the Plain of the Tower). *Eochaidh* was killed. The vanquished *Firbolg* were chased to and allowed to stay in western Ireland, where the ruins of their great stone forts remain.

There is much more to the tale of the majick *Tuatha Dé Danaan*.[193] Only iron weapons could injure them. They brought the Lia Fail, their Stone of Destiny, and placed it on the mound of Tara. Ireland's rightful kings have since been chosen when the Lia Fail called out. The *Tuatha* also carried the Spear of Lugh (which assured victory to its wielder), the Sword of Nada (from which nobody could escape), and the Cauldron of the Dagda (from which no one went unsatisfied).

After defeating the *Firbolg*, the *Tuatha* were challenged by the *Fomorians*, whom they defeated in County Rosecommon in the second battle of Magh Tuiredh. That gained them uncontested control of the land.

Eventually, the *Tuatha* were defeated by the sons of *Mil* (the first Gaels), who occupied Eire. But that didn't end the *Tuatha Dé Danaan*. They reached an agreement to live underground, in another dimension of space and time, in *Sidhe*, the invisible sites of Tir na nÓg (the Land of the Young). The Irish have honored these half-gods and faerie folk and know them as the good people of the mounds. Entrances into their faerie mounds include a famous one in Newgrange.

The *Sidhe* can move swiftly through the air and change shape at will.[194] Belief in them has not been erased in rural Ireland and Scotland. There is even a legend, the *Colloquy of the Ancients*, about a dialogue between Saint Patrick and the Ghost of Caelite of the Fianna. A faerie woman amazed the Saint when she came out of the Cave of Cruachan wearing a green mantle and a crown of gold. Saint Patrick asked why the ghost was old and withered and the faerie was young and beautiful. The Ghost of Caelite replied: *She is of the Tuatha Dé Danaans who are unfading...and I am of the sons of Mil, who are perishable and fade away.*

Folklore describes the *Sidhe* as descendants of agricultural gods and controllers of crop ripening and cattle milk yield. Their revenge on their *Milesian* conquerors is stated, in the Book of Leinster, to be destruction of wheat and the ruining of milk. A treaty made by the *Milesians* with the *Sidhe* honors them with offerings of milk and butter.

The *Milesians* were the last mythical invaders of Ireland.[195] All present day Irish are descended from them. Their legend starts with the Tower of Babel and God's invention of languages to end that project through inability to communicate. A man named *Fenius* (or *Feinas*) then sent scholars throughout the world to learn all the languages, handpicked the best one, and named it Goidelic (the precursor of Gaelic). Years later, *Fenius's* son *Neil* (or *Niul*) married *Scota*, a pharaoh's daughter. She gave birth to a son named *Gaedhael* (or *Gadhael Glas*). He was bitten by a snake and went to Moses, who prayed and touched the bite with his staff, healing it. Moses gave the lad the staff, stating: *God commands and I command that this boy's descendants will live in a land free from snakes.*

Generations later, *Sru*, a successor of *Gaedhael*, took his tribe from Egypt. They tried settling on Crete, which–like Ireland–had no snakes. After five generations of war, the tribe moved to the Iberian Peninsula where *Breogán*, a descendant of *Gaedhael*, built a tower on the northern coast. *Ith*, *Breogán's* son, spotted land across the sea. His family organized an expedition to reach it. (Famine may have been a contributing cause.) Upon arriving at this land that they called Innis Fail (the Island of Promise/Destiny), they encountered the *Tuatha Dé Danaan*. A battle ensued. *Ith* was fatally wounded. The *Milesians* fled, and formed a fleet to attack the *Tuatha*.

The attackers were led by four brothers: *Eber Donn* (brown *Eber*), *Eber Finn* (fair *Eber*), *Eremon*, and *Ir*. Sibling rivalry caused *Ir's* death en route. When the *Tuatha* saw the fleet, they shielded Ireland in mist. The three brothers nonetheless went ashore, asked the *Tuatha* to share the land, and were asked to return to their ships while their request was considered. Before an answer came, *Eber Donn* insulted the *Tuatha* and a supernatural storm arose, killing him. *Eber Finn* and *Eremon* declared war. On the way to the battleground, they met three women–*Banba*, *Fodhia*, and *Éire*. Each of these asked to have the island named after herself if the *Milesians* won.

The mortal *Milesians* won the war in two battles. They named the land *Éire*, and used the names *Banba* and *Fodhia* in poetry and oral literature. Some suppose the *Tuatha* lost because they had become weak and neglected their fighting skills. Others postulate that the *Tuatha Dé Danaan* were a bronze age tribe fighting an iron age foe with weapons that the *Tuatha's* majick was useless against.

Eremon and *Eber Finn* divided Éire into four parts. *Eremon* took the north and *Eber* the south. The southwest was given to *Lughaid* (*Eber* and *Eremon's* cousin, and the son of *Ith*), and the northeast went to *Ir's* descendants.

A common perception is that the *Milesians* were the Gaels, who originated in the south of modern France and the north of Spain, and were the last Celtic tribe to arrive in Ireland. (Gael is a shortened form of *Gaedhael*.) Some think that the Gaels are the lost Tribe of Israel (based on the family trees of Ulster's kings, on the Stone of Destiny, and on the Red Hand of O'Neill).[196]

For many centuries before the last large migration of the Irish into Scotland (in the 5th Century AD), the Irish and the Scottish Picts intermarried. That led to similarities between the folklore of Ireland and Scotland. Both Ireland and Scotland have faerie women, the most widely known of which are the banshees. In Ireland the banshee is the Bean Sidhe, the ancestress of the old, aristocratic clans. Before any family death or misfortune, she wails an unearthly lament. She is also known as badhbh chaointe, a Celtic war goddess who, in the form of a crow, shrieks over battlefields. The Scottish banshee is the Bean Tighe, a faerie housekeeper also known as Glastig Uaine, the Green Lady. She often watches over old Scottish clan castles.   A wilder Scottish banshee lurks in the woods and moors at dusk to lure travelers to their doom.

Myth has been involved in harm as well as in entertaining and educational folklore. An infamous example was the November 18, 1978 mass suicide of over 900 "Peoples Temple" members and families who relocated from San Francisco to Guyana to establish a socialist community (named Jonestown) there.[197] Another was the Heaven's Gate religious group. Believing that Earth was soon to be cleared of life, they planned to escape on a space ship claimed to be trailing the Hale-Bopp comet, with 39 of them (including six castrated males) committing suicide by poisoning in March 1997.[198]

Surviving folklore describes the Celts as having values much like our own, and to be tellers of tales with revealing embedded messages (such as too many women and heedless ventures after gold being dangerous). Christianity inevitably rejected incompatible pagan beliefs, but tales about the *Sidhe* and the other mythical settlers of Ireland support the conclusion that, while the Christian and Jewish faiths have nurtured humanity's goodness, mankind's basic nature (and gullibility) hasn't changed since pagan times.

Celtic mythology also attests to their fearlessness in battle. A large part of that was involved in the Celtic belief[199] that death was not the end of life but just going to the Otherworld to return through rebirth. (Our Hell could make Christianity's less devout followers a lot more fearful of death than were the pagan Celts.)

The appearance of the warrior Celts has been remarked upon as fearsome. Enhancing such an appearance to frighten foes obviously occurred. A more realistic depiction of what the Celts looked like is readily available to almost anyone of western European descent. That's obvious by looking in the mirror and at one's relatives. They don't all look alike, but neither did the Celts.

Most ethnic groups have myths about their origin and homeland, with the nature of the people evident in the role that virtue, courage, and goodness play in them. Celtic folklore doesn't greatly differ from the myths of other peoples, it just comes across as a more open and nurtured part of the Celtic cultural inheritance.

The extent of myth in our culture is also evident in anything unexplained, including hoaxes, tending to end up in mythical or quasi-mythical tales. Current examples include Bigfoot, Yeti, Sasquatch, the Abominable Snowman of the Himalayas, the Loch Ness Monster, crop circles, aliens, UFOs, etc., etc.

Inherited Culture Notes

As Christ's Sanctified Holy Church showed, inherited culture can involve destructive beliefs. My father's frequent comment that it takes all kinds of people to make a world applies. Human nature produces incompatible beliefs, little or nothing can be done to change them, and they need to be kept from doing harm.

My parents stressed following the Ten Commandments, the concept that a "bad" means wasn't justified by a "good" end, and the dictum that we each should *Do unto others as you would have others do unto you.* About the only issue was military service and the associated potential for having to kill. Such killing is considered right and proper, and perhaps even heroic, when accomplished as authorized to protect one's country. Not having had to do any killing, I've had no problem with any of those concepts. They're all part of the culture I inherited.

Upbringing and experience also have led me oppose funding the "free lunch" of those who can and should be contributing but are not. That has nothing to do with denying help to the needy, just with making the process fair and honest.

My parents worked hard, valued education, and fostered my doing so. After a career benefitted by that, I developed a curmudgeonly view that sees America as:

- Having imperfections like other nations, but working for world peace and rejecting unnecessarily killing those with different beliefs that do not threaten its own sovereignty and freedom.

- Being wrong in feeling guilty or apologetic about traits that all people share, and needing to realize that America's damners and condemners, including those cloaked in the mantle of religion, are very often hate-mongers.

- Being composed of different groups that distrust and mistreat each other, with the transition from one power group to another typically resulting in the new-in-power being as least as abusive in its use as their predecessors.

- Having repeatedly saved, at the uncompensatable cost of many American lives, European nations from conquest and subjugation.

- Wrongly deferring to factions and self-serving inputs that denigrate America's uniquely valuable contributions to a better world.

America's most persistent cultural belief is written in The Declaration of Independence:

> ***We hold these truths to be self-evident, that all men are created equal,***
> ***that they are endowed by their Creator with certain inalienable Rights,***
> ***that among these are Life, Liberty, and the pursuit of Happiness.***

That declaration's primary author, Thomas Jefferson, also stated:

> ***Equal rights for all, special privileges for none.***

In reality, however, we are unique and unequal. Physical and mental limitations (e.g., crippling, intelligence) produce inequality, and prejudicial discrimination adds in unequal opportunity. The best we can bestow is fair and equal treatment based on individual merit. (A related scoff is that some people are more equal than others. Another is: What makes you think life is meant to be fair?)

Our beliefs are always under attack. A Cold War example was the statement: *Better Red than Dead.* (I also heard its counterpart: *Better Dead than Red.*) But we "won" the Cold War with no casualties, and hoped for a more peaceful world. Unfortunately, the proliferation of nuclear weapons has again returned the prospect of a nuclear holocaust to the fore—in the millennium old clash between the Islamic culture and the Judeo-Christian one.

Muslims see Christians as waging church-sanctioned war against Islam during the Crusades of the 11th, 12th, and 13th Centuries, with extreme brutality and ruthless plundering. They also have western exploitation of Middle East oil as a basis for their view of us. Christians see Islam as, at the time of the Crusades, having been ruthless warriors against Christianity for centuries, and some proffer trying to take back the land of Jesus as justification for the Crusades.

Religion must be compatible with the associated cultures in order to survive, and culture determines how closely people adhere to their religions. The Judeo-Christian culture is attuned to mercy and forgiveness, and has a strong bias against killing. Islam's fundamentalists hold that killing infidels (non-believers in Islam) will produce reward in the next world, and the Muslim culture endorses and even demands "honor" killing for sins (e.g. adultery) that, in our culture, do not merit such punishment. Islamic culture and religions also closely integrate church and state and typically refuse to allow other religions in their own countries.

Our culture correctly treats other people as being very much like us, but does not fully recognize how much nurture makes us differ. We have been, for about 2000 years, indoctrinated in forgiveness and tolerance. Muslims, for over 1300 years, have accepted the killing of "infidels." Neither outlook will change, and we have the Islamic killings of "infidels" to combat.

Islam has vast wealth. Its believers pray five times a day to thank Allah for his blessings and ask for forgiveness, guidance and protection.[200] Muslim militants use ultimate self-sacrifice to further their jihad, and the potential consequences of Christian-Muslim use of weapons of mass destruction on each other are far worse than the horrors of past wars. We're very vulnerable because of the incredible cost of repeating our practice of posturing about but not really preparing for war until our dead start piling up. Examples include the World Trade Center, and Pearl Harbor and afterwards (because of unpreparedness for World War II). Our repetitions of that behavior fit the following Albert Einstein definition:

Insanity: doing the same thing over and over again and expecting different results.

Our culture deplores the Islamic use of suicide bombings, which are nonetheless an awesome weapon. But our biggest disadvantage is our increasing disregard for our own religions, whose related failures include well-publicized and long-lasting sins (pedophilia, theft, etc.). The associated individual and organizational misbehavior drives followers away.

We all hope for good outcomes. But it is folly to let hope result in unpreparedness for what history repeatedly tells us will happen. The power and commitment to assure that unacceptable consequences will fall on our attackers is our only real protection. (Weaker nations do not voluntarily wage war on stronger ones.) That our leaders have long known that readiness for war is essential to peace is evident in the following statements by our 1st and 35th presidents:

George Washington: *To be prepared for war is one of the most effectual means of preserving peace.*

John Fitzgerald Kennedy: *It is an unfortunate fact that we can secure peace only by preparing for war.*

Another reality is that churches (but not necessarily religions) try to force their beliefs on others. An example is abortion. Life, especially that of babies, is sacred to us. Many of us firmly believe that we are fully human upon conception, but that's a belief and not knowledge. No one really knows when a developing embryo or fetus becomes a human being, and making all abortion murder prevents others from practicing their beliefs. The taint is worse because Right-To-Lifers have murdered abortionists, thereby claiming a right to kill outside the law. I asked an anti-abortionist with whom I worked about that. He said that it was wrong, but that he "understood" why it happened. That "understanding" shocked me, but human nature (including yours and mine) is capable of participating in such excess.

A revealing aspect of human nature became evident when nicotine was identified as causing cancer. Tobacco manufacturers disputed that vigorously. I recall assertions that scientific studies disproved it, and a bombardment of ads showing smoking favorably. That was an initiation into the reality that, for power or profit or attention, some seemingly reputable people:

- Present lethal products as beneficial.

- Endorse unsafe products.

- Falsely tout non-existent dangers of products.

- Oppose beneficial products.

A similar issue is global warming. It's not credibly deniable to those who know about the climate of their ancestors' youth or the English Channel being filled by ice melt water, etc. But both sides cloud the issue with disinformation, and we don't know how far or fast the warming will go, or when or if it will stop. My father's belief about the profiteering involved in such matters (and about gossip) was: *don't believe anything you hear or read, and only half of what you see.*

Church and parental inputs taught me that we all have the potential for both good and bad. A verse from the Rubaiyat of Omar Khayaám expresses that well:[201]

> *I sent my soul through the Invisible,*
> *Some letter of that After-Life to spell:*
> *And by and by my Soul return'd to me,*
> *And answer'd 'I Myself am Heav'n and Hell.'*

Another relevant cultural contribution is the Martin Luther King, Jr. statement that:

> *I have a dream that my four little children will one day live in a nation*
> *where they will not be judged by the color of their skin,*
> *but by the content of their character.*

Knowingly or not, we each foster or inhibit the potentially lethal consequences of differences between people. Those most successful at fostering good build on the vast amounts of that done by our so many imperfect individuals and groups. (Those devoted to combating man's evil have a less satisfying task.) In addition, each of us has inherited and developed a personal culture. We pass it on by precept and example, with example being far more effective.

Society victimizes people, often with the villains deliberately ignoring the implications of their behavior, by open denigration of groups other than their own. The military has so often been so vilified (e.g., Vietnam Veterans being spit upon by their "countrymen") that it can serve as an example. This centuries-old problem was well documented in *Tommy*, a poem by famed author

Rudyard Kipling (1865-1936) about the British soldier. (Tommy is the British counterpart to America's GI Joe.)   The ending lines of that Kipling poem are:

For it's Tommy this, an Tommy that, an' "Chuck him out, the brute!"
But it's "Savior of 'is country" when the guns begin to shoot;
An' it's Tommy this, an' Tommy that, an' anything you please;
An' Tommy ain't a bloomin' fool–you bet that Tommy sees!

Victims of prejudicial discrimination feel it deeply, no matter how sophisticated the rationales. Whether they be from the wrong side of the tracks, or area minorities, or reverse racism victims, or students outcast by teachers and/or "in" groups or their groupies, or whomever, the victims harbor resentment that escalates the potential for destructive and even lethal retaliation. And, partisan whitewashing, before or after adverse consequences, increases the potential for harm.

Peace on Earth, including fair and equal treatment, would make our lives much better. History teaches, if we could but heed its lessons, that protecting ourselves and our way of life but abjuring vengeance is the best hope we have for achieving that peace.

It also seems appropriate to consider Historian Robert Conquest's limerick about Shakespeare's Ages of Man.

Seven ages: first puking and mewling,
Then very pissed off with your schooling,
Then romances and then fights,
Then judging chaps' rights,
Then sitting in slippers, then drooling.

The reality embedded in that humor must be accepted too. We all are headed, like our ancestors, for a less than pleasant decline followed by a mortal end. As the famous author and poet Sir Walter Scott (1771-1832) put it:

And come he slow, or come he fast,
It is but death who comes at last.

Political Heritage

This topic is included to add perspective—schools too often misrepresent political reality, and we all need to better understand how politics has affected our ancestors and ourselves.

Politics are an emotion-laden, dog-eat-dog, devil take the hindmost, reflection of human nature. My father showed us a piece of it in action when he was ferrying voters to the polls. They could get a filled out ballot and $5—or fill out one and get nothing. *Dad* wouldn't participate but never voted for a Republican. The many who, like him, always vote for the same party lend credence to the thought expressed by Walt Kelly's comic strip character Pogo[202] as:

We have met the enemy and he is us.

Our political parties come from the same populace and have the same basic morality. Politicians, honorable or not, cannot change the system. Each party pursues its own agenda. Supporters get undeserved breaks; others get unfair discrimination. (Rewarding victims is no remedy: unearned rewards take our self-respect.[203]) We're also stuck with our party's whole platform and with disregard of all of the opposition's, though parts of both are worthwhile.

My father saw Democrats as labor's champion and Republicans as management's (a valid view if we realize that politicians represent themselves first). *Dad's* refusal of unemployment made him less a Democrat than he thought, but we still grew up with a Democratic Party bias. My brother and I share: our father's stubbornness; a distaste for politic "yes men;" and a belief that political polarization bodes ill for internal peace in America. And, my Navy service and his in the Coast Guard show our acceptance of military might as a political instrument—a widely recognized role aptly described by former Chinese dictator Mao Zedong (Chairman Mao) as:

Politics is war without bloodshed while war is politics with bloodshed.

War typically occurs because lesser measures fail or are less profitable. It began our country and has kept it free. But its horrors separate us, too simplistically, into bellicose hawks and pacifist doves. Another oversimplification is that the majority rules and we must support the wars that our elected officials find necessary. There's no hard and fast answer here. Each war is a case-specific decision.

Some see the American Dream as the chance to get ahead through ability and hard work, others see it as a socialistic, utopian entitlement to services without regard to effort. Health care is an example. Those with and those without it have unequal opportunity to life, liberty and the pursuit of happiness. (So do those with unequal incomes or different educations.) But free health care for some is unequal treatment of those who pay for it. Limiting health care based on age is an inequality too—at any age. Further, unearned rewards remove incentive. Some surmount that. Others become dependent. That's a form of bondage, with the master being a naturally growth- and power-hungry government[204] able to prevent its victims from obtaining redress from wrongs. (Appealing a government decision to the government resembles a chicken trying to get out of a coop made by a fox and guarded by his hungry kin.)

Careful cost control or bipartisan agreement hasn't been a part of health care, and much future cost reputedly will be covered by a "campaign promise" to eliminate medical fraud (which needs correction with or without a new health care plan). A key to any entitlement is its affordability. Unfortunately, the intricacies of government financing, here and abroad, hide costs and bring to mind a famous verse by Sir Walter Scott:

Oh what a tangled web we weave,
When first we practise to deceive!

But we can still estimate health care costs because European-style care means similar costs. England, for example, has an Income Tax, a National Insurance Tax (for pensions and health care), and a Value Added Tax (VAT). A comparison of 2009 incomes for single persons under age 65 with no capital gains follows.[205]

U.S. Gross Income ($US)	Taxable Amt. after the Std. $5700 Deduction	Federal Tax (IRS Pub. 17 Tables)	FICA Tax (6.2% up to $106,800 gross income)	Health Insurance & Copay cost (est.)	Net Income ($US)	Net Income (%)
$25,000	$19,300	$2,481	$1,550	$4,000	$16,969	67.9%
$50,000	$44,300	$7,269	$3,100	$4,000	$35,631	71.3%
$75,000	$69,300	$13,519	$4,650	$4,000	$52,831	70.4%
$100,000	$94,300	$20,131	$6,200	$4,000	$69,669	69.7%
$125,000	$119,300	$24,733	$6,622	$4,000	$89,645	71.7%
$150,000	$144,300	$31,733	$6,622	$4,000	$107,645	71.8%
$300,000	$294,300	78,938	$6,622	$4,000	$210,440	70.1%

Note: Health costs represent a higher percent of income for low income individuals, who are less likely to choose or be able to pay for health insurance.

UK Gross Income ($US)	Taxable Amt.	UK Tax: 20% for <$57,645 40% over	Nat'l Health Ins.	VAT[206] (% − $) of Disposable Income	Net UK Income ($US)	Net UK %	Net US %
$25K	$15,020	$3,004	$1,778	12%, $2,426	$19,392	77.6	67.9
$50K	$40,020	$8,004	$4,528	11.5%,$4,309	$33,159	66.3	71.3
$75K	$65,020	$14,479	$6,560	11%, $5,936	$48,025	64.0	70.4
$100K	$90,020	$24,479	$6,810	10.5%,$7,215	$61,496	61.5	69.7
$125K	$115,020	$34,479	$7,060	10%, $8,346	$75,115	60.1	71.7
$150K	$140,020	$44,479	$7,310	9.5%, $9,330	$88,881	59.3	71.8
$300K	$290,020	$104,479	$8,810	6%, $11,203	$175,508	58.5	70.1

Note: In April 2010, the UK $9980 deduction was eliminated above £100,000 (~$154,000).

These tables can be used to compare England's and our costs. For example, a $75,000 gross income represents a 2009 net income of $48,025 in the UK and $52,831 in the U.S. So the new health care plan adds roughly $4800 to the costs a single, under 65 U.S. taxpayer making $75,000 a year is paying in federal taxes, social security tax, and health care costs. Moreover, Britain's revenue scheme is inadequate: their prime minister has declared: *The simple fact is that we are living dangerously beyond our means.*[207]

The UK VAT[208] is 17.5% on goods and services except food, books, newspapers, magazines, young children's clothing, and items like equipment for the disabled. A reduced VAT of 5% is levied on domestic fuel or power.[209] That VAT is not inherently unfair, but its magnitude substantially impacts UK consumer buying power. Moreover, the UK raised its VAT to 20% on

January 4, 2011. That's a 14% increase (2.5%/17.5%) in the VAT. The UK overall financial plan is to raise £13 billion (over $20 billion U.S.) with the VAT increase, to also cap housing benefits, and to also reduce government benefits by £11 billion (over $17 billion U.S.) to address their £149 billion (over $230 billion U.S.) deficit.[210]

Median household income is $34,000 in England and $52,029 in the United States.[211] England has ~61,414,000 residents and the United States has ~304,060,000.[212] The 2009 U.S. deficit was $1.42 trillion, with a 2010 "estimated" deficit of $1.17 trillion.[213] (Our "estimated" deficit is typically too low.) The tables in this section represent only a partial comparison between the USA and the UK, but England has about one-fifth our population and about one-fifth our annual deficit. The UK deficit is more onerous because the UK household has ~35% less income.

Going to UK-like health care necessitates more U.S. revenue. Taxation is one way to do that. Increased medicare charges, decreased social security benefits and/or increased FICA tax, not authorizing expensive health care treatments, etc., may be undertaken too–affecting everyone.

Lower income voters prefer politicians who soak the better off financially, and the financially better off prefer politicians who oppose free entitlements for the less well off. Another reality is that both major U.S. political parties, when in power, spend vast sums that we do not have, and our enormous national debt is irresponsible. Every year we spend more to pay the interest on it, ignoring the fact that, like individuals, government must pay its bills or go bankrupt, or have inflation do the dirty work–hitting the fixed income population the most.

For a short time during the Clinton administration, we did take in more revenue than we spent. Politicians and the media then discussed how to spend the "surplus," with no evident consideration of using it to pay down the debt. That makes it hard to predict a good future for America, especially when the UK example shows them to be in severe financial straits.

Health care ended up in a gigantic bill that the people haven't been able to read and understand. Not having had its provisions stated clearly and succinctly is harmful–in the sense that President James Madison expressed as:

> *It will be of little avail to the people that the laws are made by people*
> *of their own choice if the laws be so voluminous that they cannot be read,*
> *or so incoherent that they cannot be understood.*

Health care, social security, medicare, welfare. etc. do good but lack financial soundness. Social security even looks disturbingly like a government-run Ponzi scheme.[214] And, our real choice is to limit entitlements to what we can afford–or wait for the roof to cave in.

Capitalism has been a core of success in the U.S. and elsewhere (e.g., China). Socialism[215] has few if any long-term successes. Still, inequitable socialistic entitlements are repeatedly proposed. Quick gratification is the lure: politicians get power and the entitled get something for nothing (temporarily). An apt description of this situation is evident in statements by two worthy Englishmen awarded the Nobel Prize for Literature, Sir Winston Churchill (an obvious capitalist) and George Bernard Shaw (a dedicated socialist):

Churchill: *The inherent vice of capitalism is the unequal sharing of blessings; the inherent vice of socialism is the equal sharing of miseries.*

Shaw: *A government policy to rob Peter to pay Paul can be assured of the support of Paul.*

Our government assures safety and security and freedom that isn't achievable in much of the rest of the world. Still, we need to consider both its good and bad aspects in determining the trust we give it. President James Madison's perspective on that was shown in the following two statements:

The essence of government is power; and power,
lodged as it must be in human hands, will ever be liable to abuse.

The truth is that all men having power ought to be mistrusted.

Government restricts our freedom by using and extending its powers. That was addressed in the U.S. Constitution. It prescribed the rights of the people, and supposedly provided a balance of power in three government branches: a law-making (legislative) one, an implementing (executive) one, and the judiciary. But the president became a standard bearer for his party, working with it to foster their agenda. Courts became biased–based on who chose their judges. Even Supreme Court Justices are selected to further a political agenda. That links all three branches, making the balance of power concept deeply flawed.

There is a plenitude of argument, much of it by the judiciary, that there are many ways to apply the Constitution.[216] That boils down to the rationale that whatever the judiciary does is OK. When combined with executive orders and laws that restrict people in ways not prescribed by the Constitution, government enables itself to modify our rights without changing (amending) a single word in the Constitution that grants them. Government just changes the words' meanings. That dishonesty can make the people's rights a matter of current government whim, and allows the judiciary to supersede the Constitution.

Sometimes, the people fight back. Using sources that sell goods and services, illegally if necessary or more profitably, they give short shrift to overly restrictive laws. Alcoholic beverages are an example. Their consequences and the Temperance movement brought about Prohibition. People defied it by drinking alcohol illegally. In-your-face disrespect for government was obvious. Criminals were enriched. Police and judges were corrupted. Speakeasies outnumbered the bars they replaced. Finally, Prohibition was repealed.[217]

We now have an analogous problem: efforts to eradicate illegal drugs have been futile. But politicians present the false hope that we can make illegal drug dealers follow laws that take away their livelihood and power. That not only will not happen, it deflects attention from the core problem. Making the sale of illegal drugs unprofitable is the only way to stop illegal drug sales.

A related issue is gun control. Drug-related violence is cited as a rationale for disarming us. But guns can only be taken away from the law-abiding, making them more vulnerable to violence. Criminals will re-arm and have the advantage of their victims being unarmed. Still, gun control proponents aver that we can take illegal guns away from those using them to protect the illegal drugs that we can't get off the street. So they put our right to bear arms under continual challenge, despite clear evidence that it has been regarded as vital by our leaders, including George Washington, Thomas Jefferson, Alexander Hamilton, James Madison, and others.[218] Telling statements about that were made by James Madison, the Constitution's primary architect, and Thomas Jefferson, the primary author of the Declaration of Independence:

Madison: *Americans have the right and advantage of being armed–unlike the citizens of other countries whose governments are afraid to trust the people with arms.*

Jefferson: *No free man shall ever be debarred the use of arms. The strongest reason for the people to retain the right to keep and bear arms is, as a last resort, to protect themselves against tyranny in government.*

Deciding that the people should not be armed is proper if it was never proper for them to be armed, or if human nature has so changed for the worse that it is now wrong for them to be armed. Neither of those premises is rationally supportable.

A wise old saying (by Lord Acton) is: *power corrupts, absolute power corrupts absolutely.* It follows that armed power is not in the unarmed's interest. There are many examples of people being disarmed (e.g., ostensibly for safety) and then killed. (See Appendices 2 and 4.) Even if the disarming were initially honest, history shows that the eventual result is abuse like summary imprisonment and execution, and even genocides that kill far more people than armed warfare alone.

The right to bear arms is different from doing so. Only those who can properly safeguard and use guns should have one–they're dangerous to those who cannot or do not bear them responsibly (and to bystanders). If and when gun control is properly focused on illegal and/or irresponsible firearms use, supportable control measures can become practical. But taking away responsible gun owners' weapons because criminals use weapons illegally punishes those doing no wrong for the crimes of those who do–and prevents reasonable self-defense. Moreover, if disarming our populace can be done safely and reliably, we should also disarm our police because they would have no need to carry guns either. That disarming the police has not been seriously proposed is strong evidence of an underlying awareness that banning guns will not achieve the touted result.

A lack of objectivity is part of the problem. We could, for example, try to get an objective review of the reported[219] low incidence of gun crime in the well-armed Swiss people to show how widespread gun ownership actually works there. There's also the matter of how well gun control can work. In China, where gun control is extreme, 65 children were killed during March, April and May of 2010 (most or all knifings).[220] There are also bombs, mob violence, poison, etc. to assess. But, instead of objective analysis, we have ideologues whipping up support for their views, with the voters becoming polarized and voting the party line. It's more traditional politics, with parties pursuing only their own agendas.

Yet another aspect of politics is overemphasis on who said what in place of the merit of what was said. But "good" sources can be wrong and "bad" ones right. For example, the National Rifle Association is regarded by many as being overly pro-gun and therefore bad. But its statement that *If guns are outlawed, only outlaws will have guns* has so much obvious validity that discounting it because of the source amounts to improper rejection of a very important consideration.

A nation's political actions are a measure of the merit of its government. Our Constitution is often cited as a seminal document attesting to America's goodness. But our democracy didn't begin or grow nobly. We gained our independence through war brought about by oppression by England. Then we emulated our mother country by expanding through government-sponsored and accomplished conquest and oppression–from Indian displacement through means like those applied to Delmarva's Indians to forced relocation and warfare. The Manifest Destiny[221] concept was invented to justify taking Mexican land (Texas, California). But America then shifted toward a posture that its Scotch-Irish President William McKinley (1843-1901) described as:

The mission of the United States is one of benevolent assimilation.

Today's America is the foremost proponent of the right to self-determination that doesn't hazard that right elsewhere. But we're still maligned internationally for imperialism, even in England–its primary practitioner and the country that taught and did it to us. A more realistic perspective is that, within the constraints imposed by society and their own sense of fairness, men compete to improve their lot. Those prevented from doing so shed blood and use war to gain their ends. Some others do that solely for profit or power. That's why our world has been shaped by conflict and warfare and conquest and killing. Our nation's fight to change that is evident in the following well-stated expression of America's present world role,[222] made by then U.S. Secretary of State Colin L. Powell in response to the scapegoating criticism practiced by other countries:

> *Far from being the Great Satan, I would say that we are the Great Protector. We have sent men and women from the armed forces of the United States to other parts of the world throughout the past century to put down oppression. We defeated Fascism. We defeated Communism. We saved Europe in World War I and World War II. We were willing to do it, glad to do it. We went to Korea. We went to Vietnam. All in the interest of preserving the rights of people.*
>
> *And when all those conflicts were over, what did we do? Did we stay and conquer? Did we say, "OK, we defeated Germany. Now Germany belongs to us? We defeated Japan, so Japan belongs to us?" No. What did we do? We built them up. We gave them democratic systems which they have embraced totally to their soul. And did we ask for any land? No, the only land we ever asked for was enough land to bury our dead. And that is the kind of nation we are.*

The way to world peace is astronomically difficult. It slips further and further away because, by very strong nature and very strong nurture, we go forth and multiply, increasing competition, confrontation, conflict, homicide, warfare, and genocide. (China mandated a highly unpopular one-child per family program,[223] but the other 80% of the world typically fosters overpopulation.) Mankind's increasing numbers damage the environment (e.g., by habitat destruction). Overpopulation fosters killing and starvation that only temporarily impacts population growth (the food supply remains the real limit). And nothing effective has been done to halt the surge.

Prejudicial discrimination is another political football. It can be good, as when one does not eat potentially tainted food. But it can involve great harm, and the more civilized among us practice such aspects less, and less severely. Still, we all have the same inherent nature, one that accepts direct contradiction.[224] And, we all, to some degree, practice and are the victims of unfair discrimination. There are many examples of that. Reverse racism and "diversity" can sacrifice equal opportunity and fuel retaliation. Substituting institutionally preferred persons for duly selected ones[225] can contribute too. But intentional murder is the worst aspect. It killed 490,000 people in 2004.[226] Three years of that kills more people than America has lost in all its wars in over 200 years. (See Appendix 4.)

Public and organizational prejudicial discrimination have decreased in America, mostly from one generation to the next. Personal lives still remain generally separate. And, groups still regard other groups as less worthy. Wrongful behavior sometimes results and is rationalized as OK because "we're the good guys."

Racism can surface in terms like coon, nigger, honkie, whitey, chink, gook, kike, hebe, spic, wetback, and white trash–offensive words that focus on differences between people. An example of such prejudice (and interracial fear) ballooning into murder occurred when a new Civil War military draft went into effect in New York City in July 1863. Most of the city's Irish, themselves victims of severe prejudice, were out of work and unable to pay the $300 needed to avoid the draft. They had been repeatedly told that the war had become a fight to free "Negro" slaves (non-citizens who couldn't be drafted) and that freed slaves would flood the cities, work for next to nothing, and deprive white workers of any chance of getting jobs. For three days these Irish (and some Germans) rioted. They looted businesses employing "Negroes," killed policemen and private citizens, murdered uniformed soldiers, attacked the mayor's house, and burned a "colored" orphanage. "Negroes" were hanged or burned alive or beaten to death.[227] (Colonel Scarburgh's 1659 Seaside War had a similar potential.)

Yet another political football is illegal aliens. The meaning of "illegal" is ignored, at least in part to court the Hispanic vote, by not enforcing immigration law. Costs to the legal system, school system, medical system, etc. also are ignored. On the other side is the reality that illegal aliens perform necessary functions and earn U.S. dollars while doing so. Making that legal and fairly taxing the earnings to support the costs hasn't been addressed. Ideologues declare that all illegals should be thrown out; their opponents declare that they should all be given amnesty. Both our citizens and the "illegal" aliens deserve better. But that won't happen unless we identify the profiteers and eliminate their profits.

Our politicians also exploit the partisanship that let *Tom Bowden's* killers off and blamed the non-violent Sanctified Church for his death. For example, during the Clinton (Democratic) administration budget "surplus," Republicans alleged that the president didn't control the economy, business did. Then, when the economy became a problem in the following Bush (Republican) administration, Republicans blamed the Clinton administration. When the Democratic Obama administration then came in, it blamed the economy on the Bush administration for well over a year after taking power. That tactic works because we want to believe in our leaders and in our own choices, and do not hold the politicians or ourselves accountable. Some partisans even attack the opposition when a wrong by their own party becomes apparent. "But look at what so-and-so (an opposition politician) did!" is a typical one-wrong-justifies-another approach partisans use to avoid considering whether their own party should be taken to task.

Our long-term ancestry has been primarily a hunter-gatherer one involving hand-to-mouth living conditions. Even after agriculture permitted a longer term outlook, a strong preference for immediate reward over the prospect for a later and better one fostered a similar, widespread, paycheck-to-paycheck life style. So we're particularly vulnerable to manipulation that offers immediate reward, even when the long-term implications are dire. And, a naturally power hungry government will take advantage of that to the point of jeopardizing its own existence.

It has long been held that politics (and therefore government) is a dirty business. But it has good aspects too, and rather than bemoaning the bad ones, we should all consider heeding the following Omar Khayaám wisdom.[228]

> *...The bird of time has but a little way*
> *To fly—and Lo! The bird is on the wing...*
>
> *Ah! Make the best of what we yet may Spend,*
> *Before we too unto dust descend,*
> *Dust unto dust and under dust to lie,*
> *Sans wine, sans song, sans singer and sans End.*

An equally valid perspective, especially for the no longer young, is expressed in the following Irish Proverb:

> *Do not resent growing old. Many are denied the privilege.*

Such perspectives, and religion, can alleviate the misery of our utopian trek, behind the Judas Goats of unfunded entitlements and unpaid debt, into Poverty's Slaughterhouse.

Appendix 1: Kinship Beyond The Family Surname

This sample is of surnames incorporated in my family by marriage, those of my 15 high school classmates, some from my mother's family, and some other Rural Delmarva surnames. The Rural Delaware names show intermingled English, Germanic, Irish, Scotch, and Welsh roots.

NAME	WHERE	SOURCE	FIRST FOUND
Delmarva Surname Sources and Origins[229]			
Adams	England	From "Adam," which comes from the Latin "Adamus," meaning "earth." An early Gaelic form was M'Adhainh."	At Keynemund, in ancient times
	Ireland		?
Baker	England	Old English baecere (baker)	In Durham (in very ancient times)
	Germany	Beck (baker, in German)	In East Prussia and Livonia
Beech	England	"Beche." Old English: beech, or stream	In Hertfordshire
Benningfield	England	Anglo-Saxon keeper of an animal pound	In Bedfordshire (in early times)
Benson	Scotland	Ancient Latin "Benedictus" (blessed)	In Lancashire, in ancient times
Birch	England	Birce (Old English for birch)	In Lancashire (<1066)
	Germany	?	In early medieval Bohemia
Bishop	England	Bishop (Anglo-Saxon)	In Worcestershire (<1066)
Bowden	England	Bowden (curved hill)	In Cheshire, in very early times
	Scotland	Bowden	As Viking Settlers in Roxburghshire during the Middle Ages
Brown	England	Old French & Middle English "brun" (brown). May also come from Germanic names like Brunwine or Brungar.	In very early Cumberland
	Scotland		~1066 (the Norman Conquest)
Bull	England	Old English "bula" (bull)	In Somerset, in ancient times
Bunting	Germany	Possibly derived from the songbird named Bunting, or from a place where those songbirds abounded. Also might be from a Frisian-Lower Saxon name, or derived from "Bunt," from the German "bund," a noun form of "binden" (to tie).	In Austria
	Scotland		In Peebleshire, in very ancient times

Delmarva Surname Sources and Origins[229]			
NAME	WHERE	SOURCE	FIRST FOUND
Burgess	England	Amalgam of Latin "burgus" (town) and "burgensis" (citizen). Became Old French/Middle English "burgeis" (freeman of a fortified town). In Irish Gaelic, it can be written as "Brugha."	In Sussex, >1066, from Normandy
	Ireland		Generally came across to County Wexford from England;
Burton	England	The name for a town on a hill, or a town in an area where burrs grow.	In Yorkshire, in 1066
Campbell	Scotland	Gaelic "cam" (crooked) and "Buell" (mouth); also can mean crooked smile.	In Argyllshire, in early times
Cannon	Ireland	Gaelic "O Cainan," from "cano" (wolf cub)	In Tirconnell in north Ireland, in very ancient times
Carey	England	Perhaps Carrey manor near Liseux, Normandy. Some Welsh and Cornish origins come from "Carew." Most Irish variations come from "O Ciardha."	In Somerset and Guernsey, in very early times.
	Ireland		In ancient County Kilkenny
Carpenter	England	Anglo-Saxon name from the Old French "carpentier," meaning a carpenter	In very ancient Suffolk
Caten	England	Anglo-Saxon tribes of Britain	In very ancient Norfolk
Chandler	England	candela (Old Latin: candle)	In very ancient Lancashire
Collins	England	Anglo-Saxon: Colin, a diminutive for Nicholas.	In Shropshire, before the 1066 Norman Conquest.
	Ireland	The Irish Gaelic "O Coileain"	In North Desmond
Coulis	Canada	See "Kolis" (Polish)	In Ontario, ~1900
Davis	Scotland	Among the ancient Picts; derived from the personal name David	Believed to go back as far as 1500-1400 BC
	France	The Hebrew name "David," meaning beloved.	In Brittany, in ancient times
	Wales		In Flint, in very ancient times
Esham	England	The Parish of Isham	In very ancient Northampton
Freeman	England	Old English names "freomann" or "frigmann" (both mean free-born man).	In 12th Century County Essex.
	Ireland		In 12th Century County Cork
Franklin	England	Anglo-Saxon: a landowner not of the nobility. From Old French "fraunclein." In Old English, it became "frankeleyn."	In Buckinghamshire, in very ancient times.

NAME	WHERE	SOURCE	FIRST FOUND
Delmarva Surname Sources and Origins[229]			
Gerken	Germany	North German, from a shortened given name beginning with "ger" (spear).	In Hamburg
Gitchell	England	Anglicized Geman name "Gitchel."	In ancient Worcestershire
Gray	Scotland	Gray hair: in the Boernician tribe	In early Northumberland
Gum	Germany	"Gummer," connoting estate proprietorship, or influence in a village	In Bavaria
Hancock	England	Hann (John, in Flemish)	In very ancient Yorkshire
Hickman	England	It's an Anglo-Saxon baptismal name	In very ancient Oxfordshire
Hitchens	England	The baptismal name "Richard."	In very ancient Oxfordshire
Hobbs	English	Anglo-Saxon suffix for son of Robert	In very ancient Somerset
Holloway	England	Anglo-Saxon surname connoting living near a hill, stream, church, or type of tree (hollow-way or holy way).	In very ancient Somersetshire
Holton	England	Anglo-Saxon surname of the original family of one of the settlements called Holton in Dorset, Suffolk, and Somerset.	On the Isle of Wight, in very ancient times
Hudson	England	Anglo-Saxon: derived from "Hudd," an informal term for Hugh and for Richard	In very ancient Yorkshire
Johnson	England	"John," from the Hebrew "Johanan," meaning "Jehovah has favored."	In Lincolnshire, ~1066
	Scotland		In Dumphries
Jones	England	same as "Johnson"	In Lincolnshire, in 1275
	Wales		In very ancient Denbighshire
Kolis (Spoken as KO-leese)	Poland	From the noun Kol or the verb Kolnac, or the name Nicolaus (the conquering people); or the German name Kohl.	Unknown. In 1990, of the 361 Polish citizens named Kolis, 138 were in Skierniewice.
Kolis	England	A Germanic name brought to England with the 1066 Norman Conquest	In Derbyshire
Kulas	Poland	As a variant of Kolis. Could also be based on the name Nicholas. In practice, however, the surname "Kul-" was typically used to describe a cripple.	In Prussia and/or Poland
Layton	England	Anglo-Saxon Leac-tun, a place where leeks were grown.	In very ancient Shropshire

Delmarva Surname Sources and Origins[229]			
NAME	WHERE	SOURCE	FIRST FOUND
Leary	Ireland	Gaelic "O Laoghaire," from "Laoghaire,"	In ancient County Cork
Lewis	England	"hlod" (fame) + "wig" (war). Developed into ""Lodowicus," "Lowis" and "Lewis."	~1066
	France		During the Middle Ages
	Jewish	"Levi"	?
	Ireland	The Gaelic "MacLughaidh" (son of Lugaidh); "Lugh" was the Celtic god "Brightness." The Isle of Lewis.	?
	Scotland		?
	Wales	The Welsh name Llewellyn, probably derived from "llyw," meaning "leader."	In Glamorganshire, in ancient times
Long	England	The 1066 Norman Conquest	In Wiltshire, in early times
	France	family origin in Longueuil, Normandy	in Normandy, in early *times*
Lynch	Ireland	"de Lynch," from the Anglo-Norman Conquest of Ireland in 1169.	In County Galway
	Ireland	Native Irish, originally "O Loingsigh," from "loingseach," Gaelic for "mariner."	?
McCabe	Scotland	Mac-Aba (Son of the Abbott)	On the Isle of Arran
	Ireland	Mercenary soldiers (gallowglasses) from the Hebrides, during the 13th-15th Centuries.	In Leitrim and Cavan, ~1350.
	Ireland	Scotch immigrants into the six counties of Northern Ireland (Ulster-Scots)	~1606
McComrick	Ireland	McCormick, an ancient Strathclyde family of the English and Scottish borderlands. From the Gaelic "MacGhormaig," which comes from "Cormac," meaning "charioteer."	In Munster, in very ancient times
	Scotland		In Dumphriesshire, in early times
Mitchell	England	The 1066 Norman Conquest	In Surry.
Morris	Ireland	The ancient Celts called Britons; derived from the Latin personal name Mauritus	Kerry, Galway, & Mayo
	Wales		In very ancient Herefordshire
Mumford	England	The settlement of Mumford in Norfolk	In Norfolk
Murray	Ireland	From two Gaelic names: "O Mulreadhaigh" and "Mac Mulreadhaigh."	In County Rosecommon, in ancient times
	Scotland	The ancient Scottish Picts	County Moray

		Delmarva Surname Sources and Origins[229]	
NAME	**WHERE**	**SOURCE**	**FIRST FOUND**
Owens	Wales	Welsh "Owen" or "Owain," from the Greek "Eugenios," (well-born/noble).	In Montgomery, as early as 926 AD
Parsons	England	Used among the Anglo-Saxon tribes; originally meant parson or clergyman.	In Buckingham, in early times
Pascoe	England	Cornish, from the medieval name "Pask," from "paske," meaning Easter.	In Cornwall, as early as 1279
Pepper	England	A spicer/seller of spices/pepper	In early Leicestershire
Perkins	England	"Per" ("Peter") and "kin" ("son of")	In early Leicestershire
Powell	Wales	"Hoel" or "Howell," from the old Welsh "Houell," with the prefix "ap" (e.g., ap-Hoel)	In very ancient Breconshire
Quillen	Ireland	"Hughelin," a diminutive of "Hugh."	In County Antrim ~1169
Rickards	England	The old German name "Ricard," meaning powerful/brave.	In Cheshire, in 1067
	Wales		In Southern England, ~1066
Riggs	England	The Anglo-Saxon tribes, as the word "rigge" or "hrycg," both of which mean ridge.	In Lancashire, in early times
Rogers	England	Germanic words "hrod" (renown) and "geri" (spear), combined.	In Cornwall, in early times
Rouse	England	Old French "le rous" (redhead)	In Devonshire, in early times
	France	nickname for a rosy complexion	In Limousin, in ancient times
Spicer	England	French "espice," meaning "grocer."	In Devon, in very early times
Tarr	England	Maybe "Starr," German for rigid, inflexible.	In Somerset, in ancient times
Thomas	England	The biblical name Thomas was popular in medieval Europe; it's derived from the Aramaic name for "twin" and was rare in the British Isles before 1066.	In Gloustershire, Lincolnshire, and Hamptonshire
	Germany		In Bavaria, in medieval times
	Wales		In Breconshire
Timmons	Ireland	The personal name Timothy or Thomas	With/after the 1169 Anglo-Norman Invasion
Tindal	Scotland	Tynedale, or the valley of the River Tyne, or Tindale	In Northumberland, in very ancient times
Truitt	England	From Trewhitt in Northumberland	In ancient times

		Delmarva Surname Sources and Origins[229]	
NAME	**WHERE**	**SOURCE**	**FIRST FOUND**
Tubbs	England	Old French/Germanic sources of "Theobald."	In Huntingdonshire, Cambridgeshire, and Suffolk
Vickers	England	"Vicar" (pronounced "Vickar"): a pastor. And, in Cornish, a sovereign Lord.	In Durham, in very ancient times
Walker	England	Old English "wealcare," for a fuller, who scoured and thickened raw cloth by beating and trampling it in water	In Yorkshire, in ancient times
	Germany	The Middle German term "walker," meaning a fuller, who cleaned and thickened cloth	In 13th Century Germany
Waring	England	Old French name "Guarin," meaning shelter or protect	In Devonshire, in ancient times
Watson	England	"Wat," a diminutive of Walter, an Old German name meaning "mighty army."	In the County of Rutland
	Scotland		In the Scottish Lowlands, in ancient times
Wells	England	The Norman Conquest	In Lincolnshire, at Wells
West	England	Anglo-Saxon: someone who came from or lived in an area to the west.	In Devonshire, in very ancient times
Wharton	England	Old English: in Cheshire and Hertfordshire, from the river name "woefer" (winding); in Lincolnshire, from "wearde" (beacon) or "warod" (shore, bank); in Cumberland, from "hwearf" (wharf, embankment).	In Nottinghamshire, in 1307
	Scotland		
Williams	Germany	The given name "William," from the Old German "Willihelm" and "Williem." In Norman-French, it was "Guillaume."	In Northern Germany, in the 12th Century
	Wales		In Breconshire and/or Monmouthshire, on the English/Welsh border, in very ancient times.
Woolard	England	The Norman name "Willard," from the Germanic "will" (desire or strong/hard).	In Sussex, ~1066
Workman	Scotland	The Pict name for a laborer	In the Orkneys, long before 1066

Appendix 2: Massacres of Armenian Christians

The Armenian homeland has been occupied since at least 6000 BC. It is in the highlands around Mount Ararat and has been a suggested location of the Garden of Eden. Being in Asia Minor, at the crossroads of Europe, west Asia and Africa, gave Armenia strategic importance. It was invaded by Assyrians, Greeks, Romans, Byzantines, Arabs, Mongols, Persians, Turks, and Russians. But, as the following abbreviated chronology shows, it was Muslim Turkey that virtually wiped out Armenia and its people.[230]

WHEN	WHAT
600 BC	The Kingdom of Armenia was established.
40 AD	Christian communities were established in Armenia.
301 AD	Armenia became the first nation to make Christianity its official religion.
1000-1100	Turkish invasions of Armenia began centuries of rule by Muslim Turks. Armenia had substantial autonomy, but its Christians suffered from pervasive discrimination by Turkey's strict Muslim society.
1500-1600	Turkey and Persia divided Armenia among themselves.
1813, 1828	Eastern Armenia was incorporated into Russia.
1894-1896	Armenians pressed for constitutional government, the right to vote and an end to taxes levied only on Christians. Sultan Abdul Hamid II then had his special regiments massacre over 100,000 Christian villagers.
1908	Ambitious Turkish Army junior officers ("Young Turks") forced the Sultan to allow a constitutional government and guarantee basic rights.
1909-1913	Islamic Fundamentalism increased in Turkey. The Christian Armenians were labeled as infidels. Anti-Armenian demonstrations were held. In one of these, 200 villages were plundered and over 30,000 Christians were massacred. The contrast between the educated and professional Christian Armenians and the generally illiterate Turkish Muslim peasant farmers and small shopkeepers was exploited by the Young Turks to gain peasant loyalty.
1913	A coup by three Young Turks made Turkey's government a dictatorial one. Their goal was to unite the Turkic peoples and expand Turkey's borders into Central Asia – as a Turkish Empire named Turan – having one language and one religion. (The Armenian homeland was between Turkey and its planned expansion into Russia.)
1914	World War I began. Turkey sided with Germany and Austria-Hungary. Using the rationale that the Armenians were sympathetic to Christian Russia (there were Armenian volunteers in the Russian Army), Turkey totally disarmed the entire Armenian population. The 40,000 Armenians in the Turkish Army also were disarmed (and put into slave labor battalions). These actions received little outside notice; world attention was focused on the slaughter on the French and Belgian battlefields.
1915	Slaughter of the Armenian Christians was ordered by the three ruling Young Turks. The murders began on April 24, when 300 Armenian politicians, writers, clergy, and dignitaries were jailed, briefly tortured, and then hanged or shot. Then mass arrests of Armenian men were made by Turkish soldiers, police, and volunteers (local Turks and Kurds). The Christians were tied together, taken to the edge of town, and shot or bayoneted to death.

1915 (cont.)	Next, Armenian women, children, and the elderly were "deported" in police-escorted marching caravans. Indirect routes were used to avoid towns and prolong the marches. Government "Special Organization" units attacked the caravans and killed Christians at will. Kurdish bandits were encouraged to raid the caravans and steal anything of value. There was massive raping and sexual abuse of girls and women by the Special Organization and the Kurdish bandits. Attractive young women were kidnaped into a life of slavery. The death marches involved over a million Armenians. Those who lagged behind were beaten until they rejoined. Those who couldn't continue were killed. Food and water were denied. Marchers were forced to disrobe and march naked. An estimated 75% of the deportees died en route. Most were left to rot where they fell. The survivors were herded into the Syrian desert and left there without water. The corpses and the emaciated deportees were seen by German government officials, American missionaries, and U.S. diplomats. Henry Morgan, the U.S. Ambassador to Turkey, reported: "When the Turkish authorities gave the orders for these deportations, they were merely giving the death warrant to a whole race..." The Allied Powers (England, France, and Russia) stated: "the Allied Governments announce publicly...that they will hold the members of the Ottoman Government, as well as such of their agents as are implicated, personally responsible for such matters." But they didn't. And Western newspapers, including the New York Times, reported the continuing deportations and deaths.
1916-1917	Genocide continued, with some respite when Russia attacked, and reached central Turkey. About 500,000 Armenian survivors withdrew with the Russians in 1917 and moved in with other Armenians in the former Russian Empire.
1918	Turkey attacked Russia in May. About another 100,000 Armenians died. But these Armenians were armed. They repelled the Turks–and declared themselves the Independent Republic of Armenia. Shortly before Germany (and Turkey) lost the war in November, Turkey's three rulers resigned and fled to Germany. Requests for their return home for trial were refused. Armenian activists assassinated them.
1920	The Republic of Armenia was recognized by the Allied Powers and by the new, moderate Turkish government. It included much of the former Armenian homeland. But the moderate Turkish government was ousted. The new, nationalist leader re-occupied the Armenian homeland and expelled the surviving Armenians. The Armenian Republic collapsed. (A tiny part of easternmost Armenia survived as part of the USSR.) Turkey then destroyed the Armenian architecture, libraries, and archives, even leveling cities to remove all traces of the Armenian civilization.
1939	Germany invaded Poland, beginning World War II. Adolph Hitler said to his generals: "Thus for the time being I have sent to the East only my 'Death's Head Units' with the orders to kill without pity or mercy all men, women, and children of Polish race or language. Only in such a way will we win the vital space that we need. Who still talks nowadays about the Armenians?"

Note: Turkey, a U.S. ally, is a Muslim country that allows religious freedom. Religious prejudice and atrocity persist there (and in Christian countries too), but Turkey has become a more modern and tolerant nation in the almost 100 years since the massacre of the Armenians.

Appendix 3: Andrew Jackson–A Molder of America

We can glimpse the flavor of the times of our early 19th Century Scotch-Irish ancestors in Andrew Jackson, our seventh President.[231] He was born along the North Carolina-South Carolina border[232] to Presbyterian Scotch-Irish immigrants on March 15, 1767, three weeks after his father's death and about two years after his parents emigrated from Carrickfergus (on the coast of County Antrim, Ireland's northernmost eastern county[233]).

At the age of 13, Jackson joined a civil war regiment as a courier. He and his brother Robert were captured and imprisoned by the British.. They nearly starved in captivity. Andrew was slashed on his head and left hand by the sword of a British officer angered by his refusal to polish that officer's boots. The boys caught smallpox while imprisoned, and Robert died from it a few days after their mother secured their release. Andrew's mother also died of smallpox contracted while she was nursing soldiers, orphaning Andrew at 14. He retained an intense hatred of the British.

With very little education, Jackson became a lawyer and soldier. Nicknamed Old Hickory for his toughness, he commanded the American forces at the Battle of New Orleans in 1815, was military governor of Florida in 1821, and was influential in shaping the Democratic Party.

In 1828, Jackson received the most votes of the four candidates for president, but the electoral votes were split. The House of Representatives made John Quincy Adams president: one of the other candidates, Kentucky's Henry Clay, gave his state's support to Adams. No Kentucky elector had voted for Adams, who appointed Clay Secretary of State. Jackson's "vindication" came in 1832 when he defeated Clay in the presidential election.

President Jackson was a protector of individual liberty, but a slave owner and advocate of Indian "removal." During his administration, over 45,000 Indians were relocated to the west of the Mississippi River. Also, the U.S. bought ~100 million acres of Indian land for ~68 million dollars (~$1.47/acre, as compared to the ~$0.005/acre paid for Manhattan[234]).

In 1835, Jackson reduced the federal debt to $33,733.05, its lowest value since 1791. He also was the only president to pay off the national debt (though, in its first year, the 1837-1844 depression restored it tenfold). Jackson also pressed, unsuccessfully, for elimination of the electoral college and for limiting the president's stay in office to one term (to safeguard against corruption).

President Jackson vetoed the National Bank's re-chartering by Congress in 1832 and withdrew U.S. funds from it in 1833–averring that the bank: put the country's financial strength in one institution; exposed the U.S. to control by foreign interests; made the rich richer; exercised too much control over members of Congress; and favored northern states over southern and western ones. In 1834 he was censured by Congress for the fund removal. The censure was expunged when his supporters gained a majority in the Senate.

The issue of a state's right to nullify federal laws came to the fore when Vice President Calhoun (a South Carolinian) supported his home state's claim to the right to nullify the tariff legislation of 1828 and any Federal laws which went against the state's interests. President Jackson sympathized with the South about the tariff, but proclaimed "the power to annul a law of the United States, assumed by one state, incompatible with the existence of the Union, contradicted expressly by the letter of the Constitution, unauthorized by its spirit, inconsistent with every principle on which it was founded, and destructive of the great object for which it was formed." He also denied the right of secession, stating: "...To say that any state may at pleasure secede from the Union is to say that the United States is not a nation." He asked Congress to pass a bill authorizing military force to enforce the tariff. When that bill and a Compromise Tariff were passed and signed by the president in 1833, South Carolina capitulated.

President Jackson was the first U.S. President to be physically attacked. At a ceremony where he was to lay the cornerstone for a monument near the grave of George Washington's mother, he was struck by Robert R. Randolph, whom Jackson had ordered dismissed from the Navy for embezzlement. The president decided not to press charges. Then, in 1835, Jackson became the first sitting president to be the victim of an assination attempt when Richard Lawrence, a deranged, out-of-work house painter tried to shoot him as he was leaving the Capitol Building. Both of Lawrence's pistols misfired, and he was restrained and disarmed by the people present (including Davy Crockett). Legend has it that the president responded by attacking Lawrence with his cane and was restrained by his aides. Afterwards, the pistols were tested thoroughly and found to be functioning "perfectly." Many people concluded that Providence had protected the president, as it had protected America. Lawrence was institutionalized for insanity and was never prosecuted.

Andrew Jackson fought several duels over his deep resentment about allegations that his wife Rachel was a bigamist. The marriage occurred before Rachel's divorce from her previous husband was final, and perhaps even before the divorce action was filed. (Marriages along the frontier were sometimes unofficially entered into and ended. That was accepted practice in many frontier communities.)

In his 13 duels, Jackson killed just one of his opponents–in a duel fought over a horse-racing debt and an insult to Jackson's wife. The man, Charles Dickinson, had been goaded by Jackson's political opponents into angering Jackson. In the duel, Jackson allowed Dickinson (a known excellent shot) to fire first and took a bullet in the ribs before fatally shooting Dickinson as he reloaded. The bullet was so close to Jackson's heart that it could not be safely removed. It and the other bullets he had taken were said to make Jackson rattle like a bag of marbles. Dueling wounds caused him to sometimes cough up blood and, for the rest of his life, to experience considerable pain. As president, Jackson suffered from chronic headaches, abdominal pain, and a hacking cough (caused by a musket ball in his lung) that sometimes made his whole body shake. He lived eight years after retiring, dying at the age of 78 from chronic tuberculosis, dropsy (edema), and heart failure.

Appendix 4: American Wars

War	When	U.S. Dead	Result(s)
Independence	1775-1783	25,000	Independence Gained.
Quasi War	1798-1800	20	French privateers stopped taking U.S. ships
Barbary Wars	1801-1815	35	We stopped paying tribute to Barbary Pirates.
1812	1812-1815	20,000	Independence and expandibility affirmed.
1st Seminole War	1817-1818	30	Spanish Florida became a U.S. territory.
2nd Seminole War	1835-1842	1500	Seminoles defeated. Many were relocated.
Mexican-American	1846-1848	13,283	Texas, Arizona, California, Colorado, Nevada, New Mexico, Utah, Wyoming ceded to the U.S.
3rd Seminole War	1855-1858	26	Seminoles crushed, relocated (except a few).
Civil War	1861-1865	**623,026**	Union preserved at the cost of lasting enmity.
Indian Wars	1865-1898	919	Native Americans subjugated.
Spanish-American	1898	2,446	Spain lost its remaining territories (Cuba, the Philippines, Guam, etc.) to the U.S.
Philippine	1898-1902	4,196	Atrocities. Philippine independence (in 1946).
Boxer Rebellion	1900-1901	37	Qing Dynasty fatally weakened, later overthrown by 1911 revolution establishing the Chinese Republic.[235]
Mexican Revolution	1914-1919	35	1917 Mexican Constitution and increased political stability.[236]
Haiti Occupation	1915-1934	146	As the Forbes Commission declared, Haiti still had poverty, ignorance, and lack of a tradition or desire for orderly free government.[237]
World War I	1917-1918	116,708	Over 15 million people killed. Map of Europe redrawn. German, Russian, Austro-Hungarian, and Ottoman Empires defeated. Stage set for WWII.[238]
World War II	1939-1945	407,316	The world's deadliest war, with more than 70 million (mostly civilian) deaths. Germany, Italy, and Japan were defeated by the Allies (Great Britain, the USA, etc.). WWII set the stage for the 46 year long Cold War.
Korean	1950-1953	36,914	
Vietnam	1964-1973	58,169	
El Salvador	1980-1992	20	
Beirut	1982-1984	266	
Persian Gulf Support	1987-1988	269	
Grenada	1983	19	
Panama	1989	40	

War	When	U.S. Dead	Result(s)
Persian Gulf	1991	269	
Somalia	1992-1993	43	
Bosnia	1995	12	
Afghanistan	2002 - ?	686+	
Iraq	2003-?	4300+	
Total Deaths		1,315,730+	

Notes:

1. Warfare is still the ultimate solution to human dispute. Most or all nations have gained and maintained their sovereignty and size through warfare.

2. Since World War II, war has been producing far fewer American deaths. On the other side of the picture is the fact that wars continue. Moreover, weapons of mass destruction are proliferating in cultures that consider it just and proper to destroy nations and individuals who do not embrace and practice their religion and culture.

3. The Cold War is not listed as causing any American Deaths. In it, both sides had the firepower to destroy each other many times over, making actual war a matter of mutually assured destruction. That affirmed that rational nations with a choice do not fight wars that they cannot win.

4. **Genocide deaths have by far exceeded combat ones. For example, in http://www.historyplace.com/worldhistory/genocide/index.html, over 16 million deaths are attributed to the following: 1932-33 Russian forced famine (7,000,000), 1937-38 Rape of Nanking (300,000), 1938-45 Nazi Holocaust (6,000,000), 1975-79 Cambodia (2,000,000), 1992-1995 Bosnia-Herzegovina (200,000), and 1994 Rwanda (800,000). That's one 63-year period, and includes both Muslims and Christians killed. But the number of genocide deaths is very difficult to pin down. The worldwide totals for the past several centuries (over 10 times the 16 million listed above) are broad estimates, with an intermixing of war-caused combat deaths with those involving killing unarmed people of a different religion, social class, etc. Even without precise numbers, however, it's obvious that man kills to protect his property/culture, to take the property of others, to eliminate other cultures, etc. Some of that is Have-Nots killing Haves, some is Haves exploiting Have-Nots.**

Appendix 5: Genetic Drift and Other Population Factors

Genetic drift can be seen in a one generation change in a hypothetical, isolated population in which the births are random in sex and number. The one below starts with 2160 parental families with no Y Chromosome or mitochondrial DNA replications. By families, that comes to 240 with no child, 360 with one, 480 with two, 1440 with three, 480 families with four, and 240 with five. (Six or more child families were dropped out because of relative rarity.)

Parental Families	Male Progeny	Female Progeny	Total Progeny	Y-DNA Change	Y-DNA Replicas	mtDNA Change	mtDNA Replicas
240	0	0	0	-240	0	-240	0
180	1	0	180	0	0	-180	0
180	0	1	180	-180	0	0	0
160	2	0	320	0	+160	-160	0
160	1	1	320	0	0	0	0
160	0	2	320	-160	0	0	+160
120	3	0	360	0	+240	-120	0
120	2	1	360	0	+120	0	0
120	1	2	360	0	0	0	+120
120	0	3	360	-120	0	0	+240
72	4	0	288	0	+216	-72	0
72	3	1	288	0	+144	0	0
72	2	2	288	0	+72	0	+72
72	1	3	288	0	0	0	+144
72	0	4	288	-72	0	0	+216
40	5	0	200	0	+160	-40	0
40	4	1	200	0	+120	0	0
40	3	2	200	0	+80	0	+40
40	2	3	200	0	+40	0	+80
40	1	4	200	0	0	0	+120
40	0	5	200	-40	0	0	+160
Progeny Summary			5400	-812	+1352	-812	+1352
Genetic Drift in a Hypothetical Isolated Population							

In an isolated village with only one family named Anderson, if that family has no sons, there will be no Anderson family in the next generation. The above hypothetical population changed in the same way: the 812 families without sons eliminated 812 unique Y-DNA sequences, and the 812 families without daughters eliminated 812 unique mtDNA sequences. Also, the 776 families that produced brothers added 1352 copies (replicas) of their fathers' Y-DNA to the population, while the 776 families that produced sisters added 1352 mtDNA replicas.

The number of tabulated families having the enumerated progeny would approximate the listed values, and actual populations would otherwise be different from the hypothesized one. But the table nonetheless shows what happens in any population: the variance in births inevitably increases the incidence of some unique Y-DNA and mtDNA sequences and irreversibly eliminates some others. As that random process continues, all members of a population eventually become descended from one patrilineal and one matrilineal Most Recent Common Ancestor (MRCA). (The "most recent" discrimination is because an MRCA's ancestors are also common ancestors of the population involved.)

In families without offspring, all their unique DNA is removed from the population. In other cases, failure to have a son (or daughter) removes the corresponding father's (or mother's) unique sex-related genes. But unique, non-sex-related genes would, through bisexual inheritance, be carried forth in the progeny of the opposite sex.

Random genetic drift occurs in bisexual inheritance too. In addition, beneficial inherited traits (genetic and cultural) proliferate to the extent that nature, nurture, fate, resources, etc. increase their reproduction. Examples include epidemics and plagues that kill the more susceptible victims. The survivors' descendants are less vulnerable because of the reduced incidence of susceptible genes.

Another factor is food and water. Agrarian advances have enabled an incredible human population increase, but that cannot continue indefinitely. As populations approach their food and water supply limits, competition for that wealth intensifies. Malnutrition, starvation, massacres, and genocide then eliminate the less fortunate and the less fit. (Other reproductive wealth has a similar impact, including habitat and climate, resources, warfare skill, negotiation expertise, and organizational, industrial and business capabilities.)

Some catastrophes (e.g., tidal waves, volcanic eruptions, earthquakes, famines, droughts) diminish populations based on the event magnitude and the location of the people; genetic factors have little or no impact on that. Repopulation then occurs based on the same factors as did prior establishment of the population.

In summary, we are here because of fortuitous circumstances. Genetic drift and/or catastrophe did not wipe out our lineages or our relatively more beneficial inherited traits. Our ancestors consequently were more successful at feeding, nurturing and protecting their families, at surviving disease, and at reproducing.

Endnotes

General. These are not "standard" endnotes. They include comments on why some of this work is presented the way it is, and perspectives/items that I felt could be more distracting than contributing to the main text. In addition, my explanatory/reference notes often reference internet sources, which are more readily available than reference books. (The dates listed for them are the ones the information was last retrieved.) Such sources can be removed or changed, but another online search is likely to identify others as good or better, enabling the reader to quickly check this work independently. But all references, and especially histories, require skeptical examination to discriminate between sources of varying accuracy, reliability and political bias.

1. The Celtic cultural history was retrieved from Wikipedia, the free encyclopedia on September 19, 2010 under: Beaker Culture; Unetice Culture; Tumulous Culture; UrnField Culture; Halstatt Culture; La Tene Culture; La Tene Celtic Culture; and Celts.

2. Wikipedia, Delmarva Peninsula, 4/29/2010

3. Long, Rae, *Memories of Frankford*, Frankford, Delaware Memories Group, 2003, p 1-2.

4. Wikipedia, U.S. Automobile Production Figures, 4/29/2010

5. Mariner, Kirk, *Revival's Children – A Religious History of Virginia's Eastern Shore*, Peninsula Press, Salisbury, Maryland, 1979, p 202-203

6. Long, Rae, *Memories of Frankford*, p 1-2.

7. Wikipedia – Chesapeake Bay Bridge, 4/29/2010

8. Chesapeake Bay Bridge-Tunnel History, http://www.cbbt.com/history.html, 4/29/2010

9. http://earlyradiohistory.us/sec002.htm, 4/29/2010

10. History of Public Broadcasting, http://www.current.org/history/timeline, 4/29/2010,

11. Virginia Revolutionary War Units, http://www.myrevolutionarywar.com/states/va/index.htm, 4/29/2010

12. Rew, Lillian Mears, *Assateague and Chincoteague, Chincoteague During Wartime*, http://www.chincoteaguer.com/history/map-re10.html, 4/29/2010

13. State of Delaware – Delaware History, http://portal.delaware.gov/facts/history/delhist.shtml, 4/29/2010 Also, http://archives.delaware.gov/collections/revolutionary%war%20rec..., 4/29/2010

14. History of Maryland, http://wikipedia.org/wiki/History_of_Maryland, 4/29/2010

15. Mariner, Kirk, *Once Upon an Island, The History of Chincoteague*, Miona Publications, New Church, VA, 1996, p 48

16.   Infoplease.com – Maryland History, http://www.infoplease.com/ce6/us/A0859518.html, 4/29/2010

17.   Wikipedia – History of Maryland, 4/29/2010.

18.   Wikipedia – Delaware, http://enwikipedia.org/wiki/History_of_Delaware, 4/29/2010

19.   Campbell, Josiah, Autobiography of Josiah Campbell, as dictated to his son in Eaton, Ohio, finishing in December 1885. It was published in the 1920s, but my search for a published copy was fruitless. The version that came to me was one shared by Josiah's great-great-granddaughter Sarah Filbert Parker of Naples, Florida, and appears to be a photocopy of what was provided to Vaughn Baker by Genealogist Dorothy Pepper of Selbyville, Delaware.

20.   Block, Rudolph, *The Sanctified Band of Chincoteague Island*, The New York Recorder, September 16, 1894, p 29-32

21.   The noted proneness to violence seems overstated. The interviewee was Joseph B. Lynch, leader of the Sanctified Band and a victim of persecution by its opposition. The interview followed the killing of Tom Bowden by two weeks. Block's article attributed the lack of more deaths to poor shooting – but that may be an uncritical use of the less than objective input of Joseph Lynch – perhaps because it made good copy.

22.   I was told as a child that African-Americans were not allowed in Dagsboro after sunset. The timing of the termination of that practice was provided to me in an August 2007 e-mail from Carl Schulz of Plant City, Florida. Carl, a high school classmate of mine, grew up in Dagsboro.

23.   Wikipedia - Algonquin, 4/29/2010. Also see http://www.angelfire.com/realm/shades/nativeamericans/delaware.htm, 4/29/2010

24.   Clark, Wayne E., *Indians in Maryland, an Overview*, as found in the Maryland Online Encyclopedia, http://www.mdoe.org/indiansoverview.html, 4/29/2010.

25.   History of the Nanticoke, http://www.edwinddancer.com/history.html, 4/29/2010

26.   Clark, *Indians in Maryland...*

27.   Nanticoke Indian History on the Eastern Shore, http://www.easternshore.com/esguide/hist_nanticoke.html, 4/29/2010

28.   Pocomoke Indians of the Eastern Shore - history, http://www.easternshore.com/esguide/hist_pocomoke.html, 4/29/2010

29.   Hurley, Sue, *The Assateague Indians: What Became of Them*, Ocean City, MD Life-Saving Station Museum, http://www.ocmuseum.org/articles/indians.asp, 4/29/2010

30.   *Nanticoke Indian tribal history*, See Indian Tribal records at http://accessgenealogy.com/native/tribes/delaware/nanticokeindians.htm, 4/29/2010

31.   Mariner, Kirk, *Revival's Children,* p 190.

32. Waite, Millie Brooke, *A Goodly Heritage*, (self-published, limited edition), 1999, {Page copies made by Cassandra Gerken from the copy formerly held by Howard Lynch, Dagsboro, Delaware (deceased), p143}

33. Mariner, Kirk, *Once Upon an Island, The History of Chincoteague*, Miona Publications, New Church, Virginia, 1996, p169

34. Mariner, *Revival's Children*, p188; Wikipedia, Holiness Movement. It is not clear just how sanctification was certified. Bible study was involved. The goal was to reach a state of evangelical sinlessness, with one's thoughts and motives uncorrupted by sin. There were different versions of sanctification in different Holiness groups, with some of them believing that they achieved a sinless state through sanctification, while others termed sanctification a perfection in love of Christ. In some Holiness groups, sanctification was accomplished by baptism and the Holy Spirit. (My attempt to get a copy of the "Discipline" of Christ's Sanctified Holy Church fell on deaf ears.)

35. Waite, *A Goodly Heritage*

36. Mariner, Revival's Children, P188-196, and Mariner, *Once Upon an Island,* P169-170, is the basic source used to obtain information about Christ's Sanctified Holy Church and its members.

37. a.   Gerken, Cassandra, 05/05/07 e-mail to Ebe McCabe, with attached 5/4/07 e-mail received from Robert Collins, with attached chart of Ancestors of Dollie Simons.
    b.   Collins, Robert, 5/11/07 e-mail to Ebe McCabe and Cassandra Gerken, with attached files on Descendants of Elizabeth M. Bishop, Descendants of James Henry Lynch, and Direct Descendants of Samuel M. Hudson

38. Kirk Mariner, on p 169 of *Once Upon an Island*, asserts that Joseph B. Lynch ceased to live with his wife Charlotte when he was sanctified. And Rudolph Block's article on the Sanctified Band documented an interview with Joseph B. Lynch in September 1894, showing that Joseph lived in one house and his watch-mate Sarah Tarr Collins lived in another. Also, the 1910 U.S. Census shows John E. and wife Sarah Collins, with daughters Jenny, Lottie M, and Clara A., living in Pascagoula, Mississippi. And, the 1920 U.S. Census shows John E. Collins and wife Sarah, with daughters Lottie and Clara, living in Pascagoula, Mississippi.

39. The 1990 U.S. Census shows William Chandler living in Fernandina, Florida with his first wife and their children.

40. Mariner, *Once Upon an Island*, p 93

41. Block, *The Sanctified Band...*, Section II

42. Mariner, *Once Upon an Island*, p 170

43. Mariner, *Revival's Children*, p 193-194

44. Gerken, *The Descendants of Joshua Chandler*, a genealogy record of research by Cassandra Gerkin of Dagsboro, Delaware.

45. Mariner, *Revival's Children*, p 193-194, referencing April 23, 1892 and September 8, 1894 *Peninsula Enterprise* articles.

46. Mariner, *Revival's Children*, p 194

47. The September 8, 1894 edition of the Salisbury Advertiser, Salisbury, Maryland, in an article titled *The "Sanctified" in Trouble,* reported that the people of Frankford, Delaware, enraged by the conduct of CSHC, had several weeks earlier burned the church CSHC had established in Frankford, and that CSHC's parent church had also been burned once and rebuilt. (This may have been the CSHC Church in Omar, near Frankford, where CSHC still has a church.)

48. The September 8, 1894 Salisbury Advertiser report also included a "special to the evening News Balto. Wednesday," stating that "if Joseph B. Lynch is caught he may suffer the same kind of punishment his name indicates..." and that the murdered Captain Bowden had persuaded his wife to quit the (Sanctified) Band and belonged to the Citizen's Committee that had been trying to rid the Island of The Sanctified Band. The article even described the feud with the Band as culminating in the worst form of rowdyism, with the lower class of people on the Island stoning the Sanctified Band. The article also states:

> The climax of the feud was reached on Sunday night, when Capt. Bowden was murdered as he slept in bed, along side of his wife. The rowdy element on the island had just been to the church of the band, where they made an attack with stones and rotten eggs, Every window in the building was broken out, and on the walls were splotches of rotten eggs.
>
> "The Sanctified Band" drove the mob back into the town. In returning to the church "The Sanctified Band" had to pass the home of Captain Bowden. The window of the room in which he was sleeping was up, and some one thrust *a gun in the window and shot him as he lay in bed. The bullet struck him in the head and he died within a few hours. His wife, who was sleeping beside him, was awakened by the report of the gun and screamed. A second shot was fired at her, but the bullet went wide of its mark. It was thought that the intention was to kill both the Captain and Mrs. Bowden for opposing the religious fanatics.

The above portrays what was termed an accidental death (when its perpetrators could not be denied) as a murder (when accompanied by the license to blame the act on the Sanctified Band). It illustrates the biases and potential agendas of sources and media provision of an inaccurate overall picture (e.g., one cannot just thrust a gun in a second story bedroom window even if, like the original "mob," the shooter is on horseback).

49. Mariner, *Revival's Children*, p 193-194

50. Mariner, *Revival's Children*, p 194

51. Mariner, *Revival's Children*, p 193-196

52. Mariner, *Once Upon an Island*, p 94

53. Mariner, *Revival's Children*, p 196

54. The CSHC website, https://www.cshc.org, as of 6/10/20107, listed 16 churches.

55. Mariner, *Once Upon an Island*, p 94

56. The analysis of CSHC presented here is a personal approach generally based upon training in and performance of analyses of events and practices, using (as applicable) Event and Causal Factor Analysis, MORT analysis, Barrier Analysis, and Kepner-Tregoe analysis. Descriptions of the associated methodologies can be found by internet search.

57. Mariner, *Revival's Children*, p 192

58. Mariner, *Revival's Children*, p 193.

59. King James Bible. There are multiple examples of Jesus teaching/preaching (e.g., Matthew 5, 6, 7, 9:35, 13:54, Luke 6). And, while his disciples were, or were among, those thereby being taught or preached to, there is no indication that one (or more) of them was his partner in preaching/teaching in the sense that CSHC described as 2+2. So, while Jesus sent his apostles ahead in pairs, the CSHC assertion that not preaching/teaching in pairs means that the word of God is not being conveyed is not supported by the Bible. Moreover, that assertion is illogical: it is the content of the preaching that shows whether the word of God is being conveyed, not the number of speakers.

60. Mariner, *Revival's Children*, p 190

61. Mariner, *Revival's Children*, p 193

62. Mariner, *Revival's Children*, p 193 describes the shots as being fired into the air.

63. Mariner, *Revival's Children*, p 196

64. http://www.houseofnames.com, Chandler, 4/29/2010

65. http://www.answers.com/topic/poll-tax, 4/29/2010

66. Chandler DNA Project, http://fairleafarm.harvard.ma.us/chandna.htm, 4/29/2010

67. Chandler DNA Project, http://www.edmundchandler.com/chandna.htm, 4/29/2010

68. Syrich Corporation, *The Ancient History of the Distinguished Surname Chandler*, House of Names Certificate 25363200720043, 2007; an "expanded" history provided by The House of Names, http://www.houseofnames.com, Syrich Corporation, 830 Development Drive, Kingston, ON K7M 5V7, Canada.

69. Archival records identify William James Chandler only as James Chandler. The addition of the forename William is based on a ~May 1993 letter from his great-grandson Douglas F. Chandler, replying to an April 7, 1993 query from A. James McCabe, Jr., a great-great grandson.

70. Like most of the ancestral information on the Chandler family, this figure and the amplifying text is based on or confirmed by genealogical (Gedcom) data provided by Cassandra (Sandy) Gerkin of Dagsboro, Delaware. I found her information to be very carefully researched.

71. The only reference to this William James Chandler is an unconfirmed notation. So there is doubt that he existed.

72. There are several other hand-me-down tales about Captain Joshua's death. One is that he was sailing with only his son Joshua, another that he was fishing with only his son Ebe. The version used seemed much more likely.

73. Unconfirmed and unattributed information asserts that there are other graves near Captain Joshua's, with their wood markers being deteriorated and unreplaced.

74. Gerken, *Descendants of Joshua Chandler*

75. Geary, Dolly Simons, great-granddaughter of James Lynch and Sarah Tarr Collins, hand-me-down Information on William (Billie) Chandler's feisty skill as a scrapper despite his small size; provided to Robert Collins about May 3, 2007, and further hand-me-down information provided on May 3, 2007 to Cassandra Gerken by Dolly on William Chandler's size at birth.

76. MacDermot, Àine, Early Peoples of Ancient Ireland, http://dedanaan.com/untilled-fields-of-irish-history/early-peoples-of-ancient-ireland, 4/29/2010. Also, Sandy Gerken found several Delmarvans nemed Eber during her genealogy searches.

77. Neal, Gregory S., "What's an Ebenezer?," http://www.revneal.org/Writings/shatsan.htm, 4/29/2010. According to 1 Samuel 7:12, a stone set up by Samuel between Mitzpah and Jeshanah was named Ebenezer in honor of the help given by the Lord after the Israelites finally defeated the Philistines. Its derivation is from the Hebrew words *Even Haazer*.

78. Campbell, Josiah, Autobiography

79. http://www.shipbuildinghistory.com/history/shipyards/2large/inactive/neafie.htm, 4/29/2010. The Spartan was built by Neafie and Levy Ship and Engine Building Company, Philadelphia, PA in 1900.

80. New York Times, September 18, 1903, p14.

81. Wikipedia, the 1903 Vagabond Hurricane, http://en.wikipedia.org/wiki/1903_New_Jersey_hurricane

82. MacLeod Septs - Clan MacLeod Societies, MacCabe Surname http://www.familytreedna.com/public/MacLeodSepts/default.aspx, 4/29/2010. Also, http:www.clanmacleod.org/about-macleods/macleod-septs.php, identified Black's *The Surnames of Scotland*, p 461, as identifying M'Caybba as being a rare highland name in the Book of the Dean of Lismore.

83. *Dictionary of American Family Names,* Oxford University Press, ISBN 0-19508137-4, as found on http://www.ancestry.com/facts/McCabe-name-meaning.ashx on 2/20/2008

84. J. M. Freed, McCabe Family DNA Project Coordinator, e-mail dtd 1/29/2008: jmfreed@midohio.net to gfxr@comcast.net, brunim@bellsouth.net, and vmccabe@dmv.com

85. http://www.familytreedna.com/public/McCabe, 4/22/2010 - See Group 2

86. Wignall, Alice, *Who was Niall of the Nine Hostages?,* The Guardian, January 19, 2006, Guardian Home http://www.guardian.co.uk/g2/story/0,1689565,00.html

87. *The High Kings of Ireland,* http://www.heraldry.ws/info/article12.html, p18 of 26, as of 1/24/2008

88. Family Tree Haplogroup Certificate for Ebe C. McCabe

89. Wilson, David, *Distribution of R1b1c7 in the British Isles, More Scottish than Irish?* http://archiver.rootsweb.com/th/read/GENEALOGY-DNA/2006-11/1162479813, 2 Nov 2006

90. *Niall of the Nine Hostages and the High Kings of Ireland?,* Oxford Ancestors website, http://www.oxfordancestors.com/service_kings.html

91. Wignall, *Who was Niall..."*

92. McCabe, Vernon W., Jr., *Descendants of John McCabe, 1727-1800, Edition III,* self published, 2003, author's address 9830 Keyser Point Road, Ocean City, MD 21842

93. *The Ancient History of the Distinguished Surname McCabe,* an "expanded" history by The House of Names, Certificate 25363200720043; http://www.houseofnames.com, Syrich Corporation, 830 Development Drive, Kingston, ON K7M 5V7, Canada. (This has been a basic reference on much of the McCabe surname source information in this history.)

94. a. Wikipedia, Hebrides
    b. McCabe is an identified sept of the MacLeod Clan (www.the gallowglass.com, and www.it.jcu.edu.au/~alan/genealogy.html). The latter of these references states that the MacLeods are a Highland Clan of Norse ancestry. And, the MacCabe surname is identified as an Isle of Lewes surname of the Clan MacLeod, http://en.wikipedia.org/wiki/Clan _MacLeod, 4/29/2010

95. a. Wikipedia, Hebrides.
    b. Williams, Peter N., *Scotland: A Brief History – Celtic Scotland,* http://brittania.com/celtic/Scotland/scot2b.html.

96. a. The Celts, http:www.ibiblio.org/gaelic/celts/html
    b. Wikipedia, Scotia
    c. Argyll History, http://argyllonline.co.uk/index.asp?id=20
    d. The Celts –The History of Scotland, http://www.netmedia.co.uk/history/week-4/
    e. The Celtic Tribes of Britain, http://roman-britain.org/tribes

97.   *Britannia's Guide to Scotland*, http://brittania.com/celtic/scotland/scot2b.html

98.   Mac Alpin's Treason: The End of the Picts, http://members.tripod.com/Halfmoon/pict4

99.   a.   Joyce, P. W., A Concise History of Ireland, Chapter III
       b.   *Saint Patrick of Ireland*, http://www.saintpatrickdc.org/ss/0317patr.htm
       c.   Wikipedia, Scoti

100.   A now unavailable genealogy study commissioned by my uncle (A. James McCabe, Jr.) identified Mac Caba as the Son of the Helmeted One. The Clan Knowles website, http://www.knowlesclan.org/mccabe.htm, provides the same definition and identifies Mac Abe as the Gaelic name source anglicized to McCabe. Other possible origins can be found by web search, but I included in this history only the ones that seemed more likely.

101.   http://www.sparththenandnow.org.uk/medieval/axe/442, Sparth Axe, 12/20/2010, and http://www.albion-swords.com/swords/albion/nextgen/sword-medieval-irish-bastard, Gallowglass Sword. Gallowglasses (from the Irish Galloglaich) were an elite class of Scottish mercenary warriors in the Scottish Highlands and Western Isles (the Hebrides). Their most famous weapon was a long, narrow ax with a curved blade, attached to an about six foot long pole (a Sparth Axe), but they also used broadswords.

102.   a.   The Cambro-Norman Invasion of Ireland,
             http:www.rootsweb.com/~irlkik/ihm/invasion.htm
       b.   Wikipedia, Gallowglass
       c.   The (UK) National Archives, Uniting the Kingdoms – Ireland,
             http://www.nationalarchives.gov.uk/utk/ireland/conquest.htm, (Kew, Richmond, Surrey, TW9 4DU)

103.   http://www.goireland.com/genealogy/scripts/Family.asp?FamilyID=28

104.   Saint Patrick's Day. (2008). In *Encyclopaedia Brittanica*. Retrieved January 24, 2008, from Encyclopaedia Brittanica Online: http://www.brittanica.com/eb/article-9389231

105.   *Niall of the Nine...*, Oxford Ancestors website

106.   Sykes, Bryan, *Blood of the Isles*, Bantam Press, 2006, p126

107.   a.   Desmond, Jerry, *Desmond's Concise History of Ireland*,
             http://members.tripod.com/~JerryDesmond/index-2.html, Chapter 7
       b.   The Ulster-Scots Society of America, *Immigrants From The North Of Ireland*,
             http ://www.electricscotland.com/escgi/print.pl
       c.   Our Scotch/Irish Heritage, Chronology,
             http://members.aol.com/ntgen/hrtg/scirish.html

108.   Wikipedia, Ulster-Scots

109.   Wikipedia, Presbyterian Church in Ireland

110.   a.   The Ulster-Scots Society of America, *The Ulster-Scots*,
http://www.electricscotland.com/history/ulster_scots/ulster2.htm
      b.   Our Scotch/Irish Heritage, Chronology,
http://members.aol.com/ntgen/hrtg/scirish.html

111.   Ford, Henry Jones, *the Scotch-Irish in America*, 1915, Chapter V. Available online at
http://www.libraryireland.com/ScotchIrishAmerica

112.   Desmond, Chapter 10

113.   This is evident from http://newadvent.org/cathen/08132b.htm, 3/30/2010, and in
multiple other sources.

114.   That term paper has long ago been discarded, and I didn't refer to the subway
bombing in it. The associated information is based on memory.

115.   Http://en.wikipedia.org/wiki/Participants_in_World_War_II#Ireland, 10/5/2010

116.   Paterson, Raymond Campbell, *The Scots-Irish: The Thirteenth Tribe - Ulster Ancestry
(Scots)*,http://www.ulsterancestry.com/ulster-scots.html

117.   McCabe, Vernon, *Descendants of John McCabe*, p x-xii

118.   Wikipedia, Ulster-Scots

119.   See http://www.siliconglen.com/celtfaq/1html, 7/22/2007 for an extract from Delany,
Frank, *The Celts*, Grafton Books, London, 1986. See also
http://members.aol.com/skyelander/celts2.html, 7/22/2007.

120.   Ancestry World Tree Project, Entry 36716, downloaded by Bruni Mecabe on 4/2/2004,
is a posting identifying a John McCabe, b. 13 May 1727 in Worchester County,
Maryland. The posting listed Richard Ripley as a contact. Richard and Judy Ripley
host Network of Founding Family Genealogies (NFFG) Heritage Registry website at
http://www.heritageregistry.net. Theirs is a contributory online family tree. Bruni's
identification of the Ripley posting led to eventual contact with Richard, who identified
the three potential ancestors of this John McCabe.

121.   Ripley, Richard, DFNW-NFFG Genealogical Center, 141 Perth St., Stratford, Ontario,
Canada N5A 3Y1, 2/25/2008 e-mail to Ebe C. McCabe, Jr.

122.   Ancestry World Tree Project, *The Roads Taken, Records and Stories of Our Families
(In Progress)*, no longer available, downloaded 4/2/2004 from:
http://awt.ancestry.comlcgi-bin/igm.cgi?op=GET&db=verdego&id=112777

123.   Wikipedia, *Shire*

124.   Worcester County MD website, http://www.rootsweb.com/~mdworces/history.htm

125.   Torrence, Clarence, *Old Somerset on the Eastern Shore of Maryland*, Appendix VII, p
423-4; reprinted for Clearfield Company, Inc. by Genealogical Publishing Company,
Inc., Baltimore, MD, 1993

126. Monaghan History, http://ahd.exis.net/monaghan/towns.htm

127. County Monaghan Church Registers, http://ahd.exis.net/monaghan/churchregisters.htm

128. Ancestry World Tree Project

129. Kilmore, Elphin, and Ardagh Parish, http://kilmore.anglican.org, 2/21/2008

130. This Dr. Marion McCabe is not the known father of John S. McCabe (1727-1800). He is shown here to point out that possibility and the probability that 1727 John was an immigrant. The father of Mollie Beck of Carlsbad, CA told her, emphatically, that 1727 John's ancestors were Highland Scots–itinerant Cattle Drovers who moved to Belfast because of taxation, and that Dr. Marion McCabe of Belfast was 1727 John's father. She informed Vernon McCabe, who documented that on Page xiv of Edition III of his book on 1727 John's descendants. Also noteworthy is a 1/7/1976 letter from Paul Bennett McCabe, Dagsboro, Delaware, to Steven Wolfe, based on the Bible of 1727 John McCabe, which Paul Bennett McCabe had, and in which 1727 John McCabe was identified as John McCabe, Jr. Therefore, in this history, the John McCabes in the early family are often identified as: 1727 John, 1759 John, etc. (to avoid confusion). The reader should also consider Endnote 134, following.

131. Delaware Archives, McCabe Family, Document 2, McCabe Family Bible, 1830, identifies John McCabe's lifespan as 1/13/1718-1/20/1800. That would have made his military service begin at age 58. The 1718 date was considered less likely, and this record of information from a family Bible may have been mis-typed when recorded.

132. Delaware Archives, McCabe Family, Document 2, identifies the date of death of John McCabe's wife Mary as June 9, 1800.

133. McCabe, Vernon W. Jr.,9830 Keyser Point Road, Ocean City, MD 21842, *Descendants of John McCabe (1727-1800) of Sussex County, Delaware, Edition III*, 2003 (self-published). This was my basic reference for information on *1727 John*.

134. McCabe, Vernon, p1. Vernon did not label John McCabe as John Jr., and I have followed his labeling. But, if the information reportedly in 1727 John's bible is valid, 1727 John was the Junior, his son was John III, and his grandson was John IV. That would also rule out Dr. Marion McCabe as being 1727 John's father. (Bible examination is needed to assess name and parentage correctness.)

135. McCabe, Vernon, unnumbered pages immediately preceding Page 1. Vernon's work seems more realistic in this regard than Steven Wolfe's very valuable version.

136. Wolfe, Steven, *John McCabe, Jr., Revolutionary War Veteran*, 1976. This paper was written to inform *1727 John's* descendants about their ancestor's sacrifices.

137. There was never a "Worchester" County, Maryland. Maryland's present Worcester County was established in 1742, 15 years after *1727 John McCabe* was born. "Worchester" is a not uncommon misspelling of "Worcester," (pronounced Wooster), as is evident in the Delaware Archives Online (see the writeup for Baltimore Hundred in the Delaware Markers section). There also was an earlier Worcester County,

Maryland, established in June 1672. Both of those Worcester Counties included land that is now in Sussex County, Delaware. In 1767, when the boundary between Delaware and Maryland was formally settled, Maryland dropped its claims to land in Delaware. So it should be expected to find old family information identifying locales in Sussex County, Delaware (particularly ones in Baltimore Hundred, where Selbyville is) as being in Maryland. The reference for the above Worcester County identification information is: Torrence, Clarence, *Old Somerset of the Eastern Shore of Maryland,* reprinted for Clearfield Company, Inc., by Genealogical Publishing Company, Inc., Baltimore, MD, 1993

138. The location of Mumford's Choice isn't clear. The staff at the Nabb Research Center in Salisbury, MD surmised that it appears to have been located near the beginnings of the Saint Martin's River, which runs from Selbyville, DE to Fenwick Island, DE.

139. McCabe, Vernon, p1. The middle "S." initial was added to 1759 John McCabe's name because of his son being identified as John S. McCabe, III.

140. McCabe, Vernon, p1. contains the note "? Hung himself" about this Matthew. In August 2007, I telephoned Vernon to ask if he knew anything more about that; he didn't, and couldn't recall the source. It isn't appropriate to guess.

141. Marbury v. Madison, March 2, 1801, as presented at http://www.oyez.org/cases..., 2/17/2010

142. http://www.u-s-history.com article re: Impressment, 2/17/2010

143. http://www.gatewayno.com/history/War1812.html, 2/17/2010

144. http://www.thefinertimes.com/war-of-1812, 2/17/2010

145. http://www.danielhaston.com/history/war-1812/neworleans-battle.htm, 3/18/2010

146. http://www.militaryfactory.com/american_war_deaths.asp, 2/18/2010

147. My first cousin, Barbara Godwin, has a portrait of Etta, showing striking beauty.

148. http://en.wikipedia.org/wiki/Charles_Lindbergh.22The_Crime_t...,10/5/2010

149. Http://en.wikipedia.org/wiki/Douglas_Corrigan, 10/5/2010

150. Wikipedia, V-Mail

151. http://library.duke.edu/digitalcollections/adaccess/warbonds.html, 6/7/2010

152. http://en.wikipedia.org/wiki/Displaced_Persons_camp, 4/5/2010

153. *A Brief History of Prussia*, http://www.kolpack.com/packnet/prussia.html

154. Polish Roots, West Prussia, http://polishroots.org/slownik/west prussia.htm

155. Polish Roots, East Prussia, http://polishroots.org/genpoland/eastpr.htm

156. Eastern European Genealogical Society, Winnipeg, Canada, http://www.eegsociety.org/Home.aspx

157. Surname Database, http://surnamedb.com/surname.aspx?name=Kulas

158. Hoffman, Fred, author of an e-mail dtd Thursday, May 31, 2007, 3:47:34 PM. Hoffman names his source as Polish name expert Professor Kazimierz Rymut's book on Polish surnames.

159. Hoffman, Fred, response to Mark Kulis, http://www.polishroots.org/surnames/surnames_7.htm

160. Sykes, Bryan, *Blood of the Isles, Bantam Press,* 2006. Also published, with a North American Preface, as *Saxons, Vikings, and Celts: The Genetic Roots of Britain and Ireland,* W. W. Norton & Company, 2006. Professor Sykes is a pioneer of genetic anthropology. His book was my primary source of information on my family's overseas ancestry.

161. Sykes, *Blood...,* p 2, 138-141

162. Diamond, Jared, *Guns, Germs, and Steel,* W. W. Norton, 1997, p 20-21

163. Gallagher, Gary W., Ph.D, John L. Nau Professor in the History of the American Civil War at the University of Virginia, in Lecture #7 of his course on The American Civil War, 2000; The Teaching Company, 4151 Lafayette Center Drive, Suite 100, Chantilly, Virginia 21051-1232, www.TEACH12.com. Other information specifically stating that Civil War soldiers from urban backgrounds had a higher immunity to measles is also documented at http://tv-zone.com/civilwasmeasles.html. These sources directly link childhood exposure to immunity to measles; an associated inherited resistance to disease is inferred from removal of disease susceptibility by natural selection. (Those who die from measles have fewer children than those who survive it.) And Paul Schliliekelman, a statistician at the University of Georgia, has stated that "disease resistance is well known to have a strong genetic component." See http://epidemix.org/blog/?p=15.

164. Sykes, *Blood....,* p 279-282

165. Diamond, p 99, Figure 5.1

166. Sykes, *Blood...,* p 282-283

167. Sykes, *Blood...,* p 283-284

168. Sykes, *Blood...,* p 284-285

169. Sykes, *Blood...,* p 286

170. Each of us has two parents, four grandparents, eight great-grandparents, etc. – the number of ancestors we have doubles with each predecessor generation. And a sampling of my family tree over several generations showed that the average period between generations was about three generations every century. That indicates that a

representative child of the family born in 2000 has: eight ancestors in 1900, 64 ancestors in 1800, 512 ancestors in 1700, 4096 ancestors in 1600, 32,768 ancestors in 1500, and 262,144 ancestors in 1400. People have, according to Sykes, about 10,000 genes. Considering that some of our ancestors appear more than once in our lineage, 1500 AD seems a reasonable approximation of the time before which some of our ancestors contributed less than a whole gene (the "unit of heredity") to their descendants of today. (That doesn't mean we don't have some of their DNA.)

171. Neanderthal (homo neanderthalensis) genotyping has shown that, in non-Africans, 1-4% of our species' (homo sapiens) genome is Neanderthal genes. See http://online.wsj.com/article/SB10001424052748703686630457522838090203798.html, 5/8/2010, or the Wall Street Journal 5/8/2010 Page A3 Article by Holz, Robert Lee, titled *Most People Carry Neanderthal Genes.* The actual study was headed up by geneticist Dr. Svante Pääbo at the Max Planck Institute for Evolutionary Anthropology in Leipzig, Germany. Because it showed no Neanderthal genes in the African genome of our species, the Neanderthal genes had to be inserted by interbreeding between the two species after homo sapiens migrated from Africa, and the Neanderthal genes survived because they better adapted their carriers to living in Europe/Asia. It is highly unlikely that Viking and other invaders of Ireland and Britain did not similarly introduce genes into the Celtic genome.

172. Family Tree Explanatory Data provided with genetic analysis

173. Family Tree DNA report of my Y Chromosome analysis.

174. Sykes, *Blood...,* p 157, 290

175. Y Haplogroup R1b, http://freepages.genealogy.rootsweb.com/~dgarvey/DNA/hg/YCC_R1b.html.

176. L. David Roper, (roperld@vt.edu), Y Chromosome Biallelic Haplogroups, http:www.roperld.com/YBiallelicHaplogroups.htm.

177. Tsakanikas website, http://www.tsakanikas.net/paternalclans.htm

178. Data from McEvoy et al, Ireland mtDNA.xis, Trinity College Dublin, Molecular Population Genetics Lab, http://www.gen.tcd.ie/molpopgen/rfesources.php, *Am J Hum Genet. 2004 Oct;75(4);693-702.* Epub 2004 Aug 12

179. Sykes, *Blood...,* p 289-290

180. Sykes, Bryan, The Seven Daughters of Eve, W.W. Norton & Company, New York/London, 2001, Chapter 17.

181. Lewontin, Richard, then a Professor at the University of Chicago, in 1972 tried to categorize geographic subdivisions of humans to define race. He used Caucasians (his western Eurasia subgroup), Black Africans (the sub-Saharan Africa subgroup), Mongols (the east Asia subgroup), South Asian Aborigines (the Southern India subgroup), Amerinds (the American subgroup), Oceanians and Australian Aborigines. His conclusion, surprising to him and many others, was that, though people look a lot different, they're really very much alike. His 1972 paper, *The Apportionment of*

Human Diversity, Evolutionary Biology Vol. 6: pp 381-398, has been confirmed by other researchers. Also, see Human Diversity, at http://biomed.brown.edu/Courses/BIO48/40.Human.Diversity.html and the related discussion by Wells, Spencer, The Journey of Man, Princeton University Press, 2002. It should also be noted that different references give slightly different percentages – but do not change Lewontin's conclusion.

182.   The Y-DNA and mtDNA ancestral charts come from sources of sometimes inconsistent information. The data is based on different samples and even on different models (e.g., some scientists consider mtDNA Haplogroup L0 to be extinct and place the associated data in Haplogroup L1). There's a perhaps associated difference in estimated ancestral dates – with information depicting 140 KYA as the mtMRCA date of origin rather than the 200 KYA value. Errors in my compilation should be attributed to my conjecturing, and not to my references, which included:
a. Sykes, *The Seven Daughters...*
b. Sykes, *Blood of...*
c. Wikipedia Online Encyclopedia Articles on Specific Haplogroups
d. National Geographic Genographic Project Atlas of the Human Journey, https://www3.nayionalgeographic.com/genographic
e. DNA Information provided incident to DNA analysis by FamilyTree DNA
f. Celtic Connections, http://ww3w.geocities.com/geer_family/celtic.html?200730
g. http://tsakanikas.net/paternalclans.htm
h. Wade, Nicholas, *Before The Dawn*, The Penguin Press, New York, 2006, esp. Figure 4.2, p57, and Figure 4.3, p59.

183.   Wikipedia, *Brigadoon*. Lerner and Loewe based *Brigadoon* on a story by Friedrich Gerstäcker. German mythology is not a long stretch from that of the Celts.

184.   Wikipedia, *Camelot*.

185.   Http://modern-us-history.suite101.com, 7/30/2010, The Camelot Presidency of John F. Kennedy

186.   I learned of this promise from my mother, at about the same time that my father related the story about a pot of gold at the rainbow's end. Christianity's promise of the rainbow is stated in the (King James) bible: Genesis 9:12-15, documents God's statement to Noah: "And God said, this is the token of the covenant which I make between me and you and every living creature that is with you, for perpetual generations: I do set my bow in the cloud, and it shall be for a token of a covenant between me and the earth, And it shall come to pass, when I bring a cloud over the earth, that the bow shall be seen in the cloud: And I will remember my covenant, which is between me and you and every living creature of the flesh; and the waters shall no more become a flood to destroy all flesh." The rainbow has been in many religions. It has been seen as the bridge between heaven and earth, and also has been perceived to be the pathway to the spirit world, the (Australian aborigine's) creator, the pathway people used to first reach earth (southern Gabon), the bow the Hindu God Indra uses to fire lightning bolts, the source of all the world's water (Kenya's Luyia people), etc., etc. (See Wikipedia, Rainbows in Mythology, and http://www.zianet.com/rainbow/freelig.htm, Rainbow Mythology)

187. Wikipedia, *Ghoul*

188. Wikipedia, Halloween, 3/18/2008; and http://www.jeremiahproject.com/culture/halloween.html

189. Http://www.britannica.com/eb/article-22967/Ireland

190. MacDonald, L., *Celtic Folklore: The People of the Mounds, Articles on the Sidhe*, Dalradia Magazine, 1. See http://deoxy.org/h_mounds.htm, 2/11/2009

191. McDermott, Áine, Early Peoples of Ancient Ireland, http://dedanaan.com/untilled-fields-of-irish-history/early-peoples-of-ancient-ireland

192. Cereal is called corn in the UK and Ireland, maize is called corn in the USA, Canada, Australia, and New Zealand (Wikipedia, Corn). The corn the Fomorii got was cereal.

193. The story of these Tuatha is taken from http://www.shee-eire.com/Magic&Mythology/Races/Tuatha-De-Danaan..., 2/10/2009

194. From here on, the story of the Sidhe is based on MacDonald's *Celtic Lore: The People of the Mounds,...*

195. The story of the Milesians is from the Triskelle - Irish history: Milesians website at http://www.triskelle.eu/history/milesians.php?index=060.015.010.070 on 2/11/2009.

196. As described on Http://ulsterman3.tripod.com/Crest_Motto.htm as of 2/12/2009, the Red Hand of O'Neil appears to be a biblical reference to the Isrealites crediting their passage through the red sea to the Right Hand of God. "Thy Right Hand, O Lord, is become Glorious in Power: Thy Right Hand, O Lord, hath dashed in pieces the enemy." (Exodus 15:6) The Red Hand of Ulster (or of O'Neil) relates to the story of Heremon O'Neil throwing his right hand ashore – though the legend usually says O'Neill cut off his left hand and threw it ashore. (The red hand on the O'Cahan coat of arms and the red hand on the flag of Ulster are both right hands.)

Per http://www.edwardneilsonandcatherinebanks.org, Irish chieftans would try to land on an enemy shore and the first to do so would then lead them all into battle. In this instance, Red O'Neil supposedly gained the lead role by standing up in his boat, smiting off his left hand, and with the shout "O'Neil," throwing the bloody hand ashore ahead of his competition, thereby also earning the epitath "O'Neil of the Red Hand."
It seems fanciful to credit the Red Hand of O'Neil, right or left, as linking the Irish to The Lost Tribe of Israel.

197. This event was noted, in the December 4, 1978 issue of Time Magazine (as found at http://www.time.com/printout/0,8816,912249,00.html on 9/5/2010) to have involved the egomania and paranoia of Rev. Jim Jones, the group leader and a formerly respected humanitarian. See also: Jonestown Massacre, http://history1900s.about.com/od/1970s/p/jonesrtown.htm and Wikipedia, Jonestown (as of 9/5/2010)

198. Http://en.wikipedia.org/wiki/Heaven's_Gate_(religious group), 9/5/2010

199. Http://dedanaan.com/the-celtic-spirit-world/celticdoctrineofrebirth.

200. http://www.everything.com/five-daily-prayers-muslim, 4/28/2010

201. The authenticity of the Rubaiyat we have from Fitzgerald can validly be questioned as putting an Englishman's slant on the work of a brilliant middle easterner. (Wikipedia has a relevant write-up). So taking its verses as a combination of middle eastern and western thought seems more appropriate than considering them the literal work of the rightfully renowned Iranian to whom Fitzgerald attributed them.

202. This well-know quote by Pogo can be found on Wikipedia and elsewhere. See http://en.wikipedia.org/wiki/Pogo_(comics).

203. Not rewarding victims doesn't not mean not compensating them - if the compensation doesn't give them jobs/stature/etc. that they haven't specifically earned - and especially if the compensation can be extracted from the culprits.

204. The ineffectively controlled growth of government may be an even bigger problem than man's natural quest for power. That goes beyond basic "Parkinson's Law," which holds that work expands to fill the time available to complete it (See Wikipedia), to the reality that a burgeoning and overstaffed bureaucracy will result. Interaction between officials in a top-heavy organizational structure will then increasingly replace productive functioning with "networking," destroying initiative and innovation, and making no one responsible for specific functions. Assigning a function to government rather than to the private sector makes performance of that function a non-competitive monopoly and needs to be diligently avoided where possible.

205. IRS Publications, especially Publication 17 and its tax tables, were used for U.S. tax information. Revenue and Customs Information on UK tax and National Insurance were used for UK information; specific references included http://hmrc.gov.uk/rates/it.ttm and http://hmrc.gov.uk/nic.htm.

206. This VAT estimate is based on a report released by Kelko, a shopping comparison site, about the UK Value Added Tax impact. It identified, during the fiscal year 2009, a VAT impact on the average household of 7.4% of gross income in VAT and a VAT impact of 5.9% on disposable income of high income earners. (http://www.kamcity.com/namnews/asp/newsarticle.asp?newsid=52875, 9/12/2010.) Since different sources provide different information about national incomes, the data cannot be regarded as exact. In the case of VAT in the UK, the tabulated data was arbitrarily assigned as 5.9% of disposable (after national income and health/pension insurance deductions) income to the highest income tabulated and 12% of disposable income to the lowest disposable income tabulated, with linear proportionality used to establish values for the other tabulated values. The result could be described as semi-quantitative – not really quantitative but much better than a mere guess.

207. As quoted in the October 2010 issue of *Newsmax, Page 40-41, David Cameron's High-Stakes Balancing Act*, by David Wright

208. Wikipedia, Value Added Tax, 9/7/2010

209. Value Added Tax,
http://www.direct.gov.uk/en/MoneyTaxAndBenefits/Taxes/Beginners...,9/7/2010

210. Budget 2010: VAT rise and benefits cuts,
http://www.telegraph.co.uk/finance/financetopics/budget/7846749/Bu..., 9/7/2010

211. Wikipedia, Median Household Income, 9/27/2010

212. Google - Public Date, http://www.google.com/publicdata?ds=wb-wdi&met=sp_pop
totl&l..., 9/7/2010

213. Wikipedia, 2010 United States Federal Budget, 9/7/2010

214. A Ponzi Scheme is a fraudulent investment mechanism that pays investors out of
subsequent input funds. (See Wikipedia - Ponzi Scheme). Social security tax income
is similar in the respect that the government spends it as if it were general income,
and social security benefits are paid from monies later received (or borrowed) when
the benefits are due.

215. There are multiple forms of Socialism. The kind referred to in this work is the one that
advocates the Marxist philosophy of providing everyone with their "needs" while
receiving from everyone the product of their "abilities." It fails because too few people
provided with all their needs fully use their abilities to contribute to society, and
because many people do not develop unneeded abilities.

216. The arguments include literal application of the Constitution's wording, the intent of the
founding fathers, what the wording would mean under today's word definitions, the
inapplicability of an 18th Century Constitution to our pluralistic world, etc. The
proponents of change by the judiciary do not typically address the fact that there is a
way to change the Constitution and changing it by judicial action bypasses the
prescribed method of changing it by same way it was enacted–by the vote of the
representatives of the people it governs. See: Theories of Constitutional
Interpretation, http://www.law.umkc.edu/faculty/projects/ftrials/conlaw/interp.html,
5/2/2010, and Constitutional Interpretation, http://www.law.usconstitution.net/consttop
intr.html, 5/2/2010

217. The most publicized prohibition criminality was that associated with Chicago gangster
Al Capone. But the problem led much further, into supposedly respectable
businessmen investing in illegal alcohol, etc. See
http://www.digitalhistory.uh.edu/database/article_display.cfm?HHID=441, 5/28/2010,
and http://www.essortment.com/all/prohibitionamer_refo.htm, 5/28/2010

218. Many sources of supporting documentation are readily available. A convenient one is
http://www.catb.org/~est/guns/quoyes.html, 4/18/2010. Pertinent quotes follow:
   - George Washington: *The very atmosphere of firearms anywhere and
     everywhere restrains evil interference–they deserve a place of honor with all
     that's good.*
   - Alexander Hamilton (The federalist Papers, 184-188): *The best we can hope
     for concerning the people at large is that they be properly armed.*
   - Benjamin Franklin (Historical Review of Pennsylvania, 1759): *They that give up
     essential liberty to obtain a little temporary safety deserve neither liberty nor*

safety.

- Supreme Court Justice Louis Brandeis: *Experience should teach us to be most on our guard to protect liberty when the government's purposes are beneficent... The greatest dangers to liberty lurk in insidious encroachment by men of zeal, well meaning but without understanding.*
- Mohandus (Mahatma) Gandhi (one of the best known and most effective proponents of peaceful protest): *Among the many misdeeds of the British rule in India, history will look upon the act of depriving a whole nation of arms, as the blackest.*
- Adolph Hitler, April 11, 1942: *The most foolish mistake we could possibly make would be to permit the conquered Eastern peoples to have arms. History teaches that all conquerors who have allowed their subject races to carry arms have prepared their own downfall by doing so.*
- Hubert H. Humphrey, 1960: *Certainly one of the chief guarantees of freedom under any government, no matter how popular and respected, is the right of the citizens to keep and bear arms.... the right of the citizens to bear arms is just one guarantee against arbitrary government and one more safeguard against a tyranny which now appears remote in America, but which historically has proved to be always possible.*
- Warren v. District of Columbia, 444 A.2d 1 (D.C. App. 181): *...a government and its agents are under no general duty to provide public services, such as police protection, to any particular individual citizen.*
- *James Madison:* A well regulated militia, composed of the body of the people, trained in arms, is the best most natural defense of a free country.

219. http://news.bbc.co.uk/2/hi/europe/1566715.stm, 5/18/2010 documents an 09/27/2001 BBC report of the Swiss people being well armed and having a gun crime rate so low that statistics are not even kept.

220. Time Magazine, May 24, 2010 Edition, P13 documents these "kindergarten" killings.

221. Wikipedia, Manifest Destiny, 5/18/2010

222. http://urbanlegends.about.com/library/bl-colin-powell.htm, 4/28/2010; http://www.truthorfiction.com/rumors/p/powell-empires.htm, 4/28/2010; http://en.wikiquote.org/wiki/Colin_Powell, 4/28/2010.

The statement in the text was made at a February 14, 2002 MTV Global Discussion. It preceded the reply of Secretary Powell to former Archbishop of Canterbury George Carey's January 26, 2003 question, at a question and answer session at the World Economic Forum in Davos, Switzerland about whether due attention had been paid to the use of soft power–promulgating moral and democratic values–versus "hard power." In part, Secretary Powell responded as follows:

There is nothing in American experience or in American political life or in our culture that suggests we want to use hard power. But what we have found over the decades is that unless you do have hard power–and here I think you're referring to military power–then sometimes you are faced with situations that you can't deal with.

I mean, it was not soft power that freed Europe. It was hard power. And what followed immediately after hard power? Did the United States ask for dominion over a single nation in

Europe? No. Soft power came in the Marshall Plan. Soft power came with American GIs who put their weapons down once the war was over and helped all those nations rebuild. We did the same thing in Japan.

So our record of living our values and letting our values be an inspiration to others I think is clear. And I don't think I have anything to be ashamed of or apologize for with respect to what America has done for the world.

We have gone forth from our shores repeatedly over the last hundred years and we've done this as recently as the last year in Afghanistan and put wonderful young men and women at risk, many of whom have lost their lives, and we have asked for nothing except enough ground to bury them in, and otherwise we have returned home to seek our own, you know, to seek our own lives in peace, to live our own lives in peace. But there comes a time when soft power or talking with evil will not work where, unfortunately, hard power is the only thing that works.

223.   http://maps.unomaha.edu/peterson/funda/Sidebar/ChinaPop.html, 5/1/2010.

224.   This phenomenon was described by so-called "rogue" psychologist Julian Jaynes in his book *The Origin of Consciousness in the Breakdown of the Bicameral Mind*. Jaynes put a chair in the middle of a room. Two groups were tested. One was hypnotized, the other was told to pretend to be hypnotized. Both groups were told that there was no chair in the room and then told to walk to the window and back. The hypnotized group walked around the chair and averred that there was none. The other group walked into the chair and stopped. Jaynes concluded that the hypnotized group showed our natural trait of ignoring contradictory/conflicting information.

225.   Racial and religious prejudice come to mind when discrimination is mentioned. But there are many more aspects. One such happened to me when I was appointed by U.S. Senator J. Allen Frear to the U.S. Naval Academy. I took the physical examination, was told that I passed, and was ready to attend. A few weeks later, my Senator called to ask why I had not told him I failed the physical or requested a re-examination. I explained, and learned that a football player had been given my appointment. Senator Frear quickly arranged a re-examination, which I passed, retrieving the appointment. I see this as an example of the in-your-face unfair discrimination that often succeeds in all walks of life.

Another perspective on prejudice is a tale of an interview of a young naval officer seeking selection to U.S. Navy nuclear power program training. The interviewer, Vice-Admiral Rickover, reportedly had much the following exchange with him.

Rickover: Are you prejudiced?
Candidate: No Sir.
Rickover: Would you eat cat?
Candidate: Yes Sir.
Rickover: Is your wife prejudiced?
Candidate: No Sir.
Rickover: Would she eat cat?
Candidate: Yes Sir.
Rickover: Young man, if you or your wife decide to eat cat, make sure you do it based on your own decision and not on anything I have said.

226. http://www.genevadeclaration.org/fileadmin/docs/Global-Burden-of-Armed-Violence-full-report.pdf, 4/30/2010, documents the consequences of intentional homicides. It emphasizes armed violence, but large scale homicides/massacres conducted with few or no guns have been repeatedly evident (e.g., in the Third World), as has the use of bombs/knives/clubs/mob violence to carry out intentional homicides. Also, see Wikipedia under http://en.wikipedia.org/wiki/List_of_countries_by_intentional_homicide rate, 4/30/2010

227. Some of this information is available from Wikipedia and other online information. But the primary source I used was: Catton, Bruce, *The Centennial History of the Civil War, Volume Three, Never Call Retreat,* 1965, Doubleday and Company.

228. As with previous quoting of Fitzgerald's version of the Rubaiyat, I have avoided including references to alcohol consumption, which appears to have been a serious problem that the Islamic culture and religion have eliminated or greatly alleviated.

229. References here include: House of Names (http://www.houseofnames.co), the primary name reference;
Ancestor Search, http://www.searchforancestors.com;
Ancestry.com, http://www.ancestry.com/learn/facts;
Burgess Surname History, http://www.burgesslegacy.org/burhist.htm;
GoIreland.com Genealogy Surname Search, http://goireland.com/genealogy/scripts

230. Wikipedia, [http:en.wikipedia.org/wiki/Armenia]
http://www.unitedhumanrights.org/Genocide/armenian_genocide.htm, United Human Rights Council, Armenian Genocide, 1915-191

231. Wikipedia, Andrew Jackson, 10/6/2009

232. Wikipedia, Waxhaus, 10/6/2009

233. Wikipedia, Carrickfergus, Ireland, 10/6/2009

234. Cecil Adams, Column on the Cost of Manhattan,
http://straightdope.com.com/columns/readf/715, 10/7/2009

235. Http://en.wikipedia.org/wiki/Boxer_Rebellion, 4/30/2010

236. Http://countrystudies.us/mexico/29.htm, 2/18/2010

237. Http://www.globalsecurity.org/military/ops/haiti19.htm, 2/18/2010

Index

Notes: 1. Nicknames, where inserted, are in parentheses.
        2. Known maiden names are listed separately and, in parentheses, with spouses' surnames.

A

B

C

Norman Ernest, 19, 25; Reba Blanche, 17; Robert, 13; Sarah Jane (Hudson), 16; Sarah Elizabeth (Benson), 9, 15; Stella Emma (West), 16; William Burton, 16; William James (#1), 14; William James (#2) (Billy), 9, 11, 14, 15; William James (#3), Jr. 14; William James (#4), Jr., 15

D

E

F

Polio: 53

Popeye Flashlights: 51

Potato Famine: 27

Power: 67-68, 77-79, 81, 83-87, 96

Pre-Christian Beliefs: 72, 73, 76

Produce Salesman: 54, 55

Prohibition: 84

Public School 70, (PS-70): 51

Ponzi Scheme: 83

Post Office: 3, 22, 41, 52

Powell: Gen. Colin, 86

Poznan: 61

Prejudice: x, 77, 80, 81, 86

Profit: 23, 79, 81, 84, 86, 87

Prussia: 61, 63

Q

Queen Elizabeth: 65

Quillen Surname: 28, 92

R

Race Riot: 86

Rackrenting: 27

Rat Killing: 54

Rationing, 52

Reading Railroad: 49

Religion Merging: viii, 72

Republican: 5, 16, 42, 66, 81, 87

Revolutionary War: 1, 27, 31-32, 34, 35

Rickards: Barbara Anne: vii, 46, 47; Birdie Jane: 46; Elizabeth Jane: 47; George Ross, 38, 46-48; Judy Ross, 46, 47; Leon Roy, 47; Virginia Lee Etta (McCabe), 20, 21, 22, 38, 39, 41, 45, 46, 48

Right-To-Life: 79

Roman: 27, 30, 67, 68, 94

Roundtree: Marvin Emerson, 60; Whitney Elizabeth, 60

Rouse, Judith Ann: 57

Rubaiyat: 79, 87

Russian Empire: 61

Racial Tension: 55

Rainbows: 72

Randolph, Robert R.: 97

Reading: 1, 19, 22, 51

Reed: Mark, 43; Kimberly Ann (Waring), 43

Religious Killings: 10-12, 78, 94-95

Rettinger: Lawrence (Larry), vii

Reynolds: Catherine, 15

Rogers: William H, 16

Roxana, DE: 14, 19

Rumsfeld, Donald: 8

R1b Haplogroup: 68, 69

S

Saint Patrick: 27, 75

Saloon: 64

Santayana, George: x

Scarburgh: Col. Edward, 4, 87

Schaeffer, Alexandra Hope, 58; Caroline McCabe, 58; Donna Gail (McCabe), 58; Kevin, 58; Patrick Michael, 58

Schulz: Carl, vii

Scotch-Irish: viii, 27, 28, 30, 35, 66, 85, 96

Scotland: 26, 27, 67, 68, 69, 75, 76

Sears: Catherine, 28

Secession: 1, 96

Self-Determination: 85

Shakespeare, William: 24, 80

Shaving: 40, 41

Shetland Islands: 67

Shotgun: 5, 7, 44, 56

Slavery: 1, 35, 54, 67, 74, 86, 96

Snow, C. P.: 55

Social Security (FICA): 82, 83

State Highway Department Job: 55

Stevens: Darren Franklin, 47; Dawn Lee (Godwin), 47

Strawberries: 3, 6, 43, 54

Spots: Dr., 50

Steen, Ida E., 16

Stove: 53

Salisbury, MD: 3, 5, 41, 63

Sandy Landing, DE: 14, 16

Saxon Ancestry: 68

Scotch: viii, 27, 28, 66, 72, 88

Scoti: 26, 27, 28

Scottish: 26, 27, 30, 66, 67, 72, 76

Seaside War: 4, 87

Selbyville, DE: 32, 36, 37, 48

Shafer: Woocko, 51; Collie, 51

Sharp: (step-grandfather), 19

Shaw, George Bernard: 83

Sheridan: Katherine Mary, 29-30

Sister Kenny Center: 53

Smith: Capt. John, 4

Socialism: 83

Speeding: 22

States' Rights: 34, 96

Spartan Tug: 20

Spiritualism: 20

Stillman's Gym: 22

Stringer, Dana Lynn (McCabe), 58; Emily Margeurite, 58, Nicole Veronica, 58; Todd, 58

Page 127

Y